Jaded

A True Story

Randy A. DeOrio

authorHOUSE®

AuthorHouse™
1663 Liberty Drive
Bloomington, IN 47403
www.authorhouse.com
Phone: 1-800-839-8640

First published by AuthorHouse 1/7/2011

ISBN: 978-1-4567-1289-1 (sc)
ISBN: 978-1-4567-1287-7 (dj)
ISBN: 978-1-4567-1288-4 (e)

Library of Congress Control Number: 2010918441

Printed in the United States of America

Any people depicted in stock imagery provided by Thinkstock are models,
and such images are being used for illustrative purposes only.
Certain stock imagery © Thinkstock.

This book is printed on acid-free paper.

Because of the dynamic nature of the Internet, any Web addresses or
links contained in this book may have changed since publication and
may no longer be valid. The views expressed in this work are solely those
of the author and do not necessarily reflect the views of the publisher,
and the publisher hereby disclaims any responsibility for them.

Say of me what you will
and the morrow will judge you,
and your words shall be a witness
before its judging and a testimony
before its justice...I came to say a word
and I shall utter it. Should death take
me ere I give voice, the morrow shall utter
it...that which alone I do today shall be
proclaimed before the people
in days to come.

Kahlil Gibran

A very special thank you goes to Matthew Rittberg for all his years of friendship and knowledge. You've been a godsend to both Ali and myself!

Thank you Jessica for being a friend and Makayla for all her play dates with Sadie-Rose

May God be with you always!

Thanks to all my friends and family who have been there for me when I needed them, especially Barbara Barr Conte for nearly 30 years of friendship.

And of course an extra special thank you to Aletha, her beautiful daughter, and all her other children for their unconditional love and support. Without them, this book would not be possible. They are proof to myself that there is a benevolent and loving God.

Thank You God for all of your blessings, giving me a wonderful life that I can look back on and truly appreciate.

Acknowledgments

A special thank you to Danielle Gorshein for editing this book and for giving Sophia a wonderful summer as her camp counselor. Hope to see you next year! You're such a beautiful and talented person! God Bless You!

Thank you Katrina and Bohdan for welcoming us into your home and allowing my family eleven wonderful years of peace, security and happiness. Bohdan will be greatly missed! My condolences to his family.

Chucky and Rebecca friends forever!

Thank you Dr. Jeffrey Schreiber for being Ali's psychologist. You've done a fantastic job helping her get through the cobwebs.

Anthony Randazzo for being a close friend and such great council for Ali's defense.

Marc Popelski for being Ali's dearest friend for the past quarter century.

Gail at Golden Steps for making Sophia's first years at daycare and preschool exciting and educational.

Dr. Alexander Zodiatis, Dr. Maurice Elias at the Totowa Pediatrics and Dr. Elliot Eisenstein for being wonderful Pediatricians to Sophia.

Dr. George L. Cameron at the Cameron Animal Hospital in Montclair NJ. for saving Shadow when he was ill.

A special thank you to Gordon and Delice Parent, for making me part of your family. May Gordon's soul rest in peace!

A special thank you to Ralph and Maddie Piccolo for all the years as your foster child.

This book is dedicated to:

All the women and men
who have been falsely accused
and sent to prison.

And to all the women and children
who have been exploited and victimized.

May you all find justice in due time!

Justice does prevail!

Chapter 1

On January 28th, 1993 at 3:35 PM,
At the Lexington County Court House of Waldwick, New Jersey,

Before the Honorable Judge Philip P. Edwards, (the hanging Judge to most), and a jury of twelve people considered peers, the verdict was read aloud. Guilty...Guilty...Guilty

Deliberations only took seven hours before they reached that verdict. The trial itself took a week. "It has to be karma," she thought to herself as she gazed up at the clock right before the guilty verdict was read.

Eight years prior to that very minute she had given birth to her second child Adam Jr. This was going to be the first birthday in years that she would miss of his and would most likely never get a chance to celebrate another one with him in this life.

Everyone should have a little hope that they will be found NOT guilty, but she knew that a miracle wasn't happening for her that day.

The prosecutor, Darrell Evenston, told the jury during closing statements, "Ms. Durant is a cold, calculating, manipulative, black hearted woman that does not deserve to live in society. That society would be safer without her in it." Wow! What powerful words coming from a man who had never even had a conversation with her. When he said those things to the jury, she immediately tapped her attorney on the back of his hand resting on the table, and whispered in his ear "Does this guy know me? I'd be the one safer from society not vice versa!"

She had never truly imagined herself as evil before, but the thought of being a dark villain appealed to her now. That there was someone in this world who could believe she had the audacity to be so nefarious. It intrigued her. She felt however, deep down inside, that his words were only those of a suit guys perception of a Go-Go Dancer. Talk about stereo typing someone. "Would this be literally judging a book by its cover?" she thought.

As a matter of fact it had been her cover. A false image she portrayed to the public to make money to support her children. It was her job to appeal to men as a fantasy sex object so they would believe that they stood a chance of fulfilling their sexual fantasies with a beautiful, young, sexy stripper. The more she enticed them, the more money she usually received from them. It was a game that she learned to play well.

Once they got a taste of her reality however, it was usually over for them. She had three adorable children, but what most men considered "a lot of baggage."

She never hid how she really felt about those men. She always considered them the baggage, and never her beautiful children. She loved them with all of her heart, just not their fathers any longer.

She had decided after she split from her son's father Adam Sr. that if she couldn't have "true love" with a man, she would have to settle for their money. Not that she considered herself a gold digger, she just felt, that if they wanted something from her, it was only fair that she got something in return. I mean after all, if a man is foolish enough to spend his entire paycheck at a strip club giving all of his money to the hot, sexy strippers, because he's looking for more than what he has at home with his mate, is it the dancers that are screwed up, or the lonely, horny, desperate men who turn to them for comfort or companionship or whatever?

Who knows, maybe it's both, she thought. She found out the hard way just how much her profession, was appreciated, by the "Authority Figures" and the general public.

Hypocrites!

They're usually the first ones in those places stuffing dollar bills into the G-strings of the girls.

UNFORTUNATELY FOR HER, THAT WAS where she met her attorney who would completely misrepresent her. She was sure he meant no harm though.

She had met him while dancing at a strip club called the "Village" on route 19 in Waldwick. He actually had no defense for her. She would have been better off with a public defender. At least she would have had someone who knew what he was doing in the courtroom.

It might have helped her immensely if he we're a criminal lawyer, but he wasn't. He was a civil attorney that knew very little about criminal defense.

How could that be, when he used to be a municipal judge in not only Waldwick, but in Arlington Township as well?

To a twenty-five year old girl who had never before needed an attorney, when this all began, he was good enough. All attorneys are the same she thought. They all go to law school and carry briefcases and practice law. How bad can he be?

He was very kind. He reminded her of her father because he was a Pisces like her father. And he had very trusting brown eyes. He even smoked a pipe that always smelled so sweet. He had a humble, little office in downtown, Waldwick.

O.k. so he was having an affair with his secretary that eventually ended his marriage, but that wasn't really anyone's business anyway. Was it?

It didn't matter to her that while Larry was married, he had stopped by her condo to visit and actually got on his knees at her door, begging her to be with him. She told him that she couldn't be with him sexually because she liked and respected him. But the actual truth was that she was extremely superstitious about having sex with a married man. She had never done it before and was afraid God would punish her, if she did. As it would happen, it would be thought by the mother of this naive girl that he deliberately sabotaged her defense because she rejected him. Absolutely ridiculous!

It was her own fault that she didn't have a defense. She only paid him four thousand dollars after all. Every other attorney wanted at least seventy-five thousand to represent her. And every time he asked to meet with her to work on her case, she would have an excuse not to. The fact was that she really didn't care what happened to her. She had failed to protect her children who depended on her judgment and deserved everything that would happen from that day forward.

She told her attorney right before entering into the courtroom that she heard Guilty...Guilty...Guilty in her head, but he attempted to reassure her, that she was wrong. She had just forgotten to put the NOT in front of guilty. She had NO defense. Only her, saying she didn't do, what they just spent a week saying she did.

Tears welled up in Larry's eyes after the verdict was read. He knew that his client was not the person the media and the prosecution had portrayed her to be to the jury. She might have been a little too trusting, maybe a little eccentric, but she was no criminal. She was a victim just like her daughter.

She was actually the last victim of a pedophile who had spent the last twenty-five years molesting children and was now sitting in jail because she refused to keep his secret at the cost of her own freedom. A pedophile as her co-defendant, and they would take his word over hers. Go figure!

Chapter 2

On the eve of January 3rd, 1991 Alisha Durant, nicknamed Ali, called her friend Fenton Noor and asked him if he would babysit her two children, Amanda, who was seven at that time and Tyler, who was only four. Her other child, Adam Jr. was living with his grandmother in Pleastant, which was not far from her, just the next town over.

He refused to watch Tyler, complaining that he was a brat. His grand daughter, who was the same age as Amanda, would be there at his home to play with her so she wouldn't be alone or get bored.

Ali sometimes confided in her friend Fenton about personal matters as though he were her girlfriend; however, he was fifty-nine years old and she was twenty-five. It really wasn't a proper relationship to onlookers.

She knew he was infatuated with her, but the age difference was so overwhelming, that she ignored his subtle advances.

Not to mention, he had been her sister's "Sugar Daddy" for about seven years while she was married.

He adored little girls so much, that he had practically raised Jessica's daughter, Megan, (her niece) who was close to Amanda's age.

Fenton had somehow become the neighborhood babysitter. At one time, Ali had observed him driving around with twelve children, ranging from six weeks to fifteen years old in his custom van.

He seemed very feminine and extremely meticulous to her. He enjoyed buying nice clothes for the little girls. He would dress them up and take them out shopping and to the movies.

It was suspected that he was gay, since she also noticed on several occasions that he would secretly meet with men, whom he wouldn't ever introduce to her.

He told her they were business associates and she left it at that, and didn't pry. It wasn't her business what anyone else did in private, she thought.

She felt that if all these other women, in her neighborhood, trusted him as much as they did, with their children, she could trust him as well. Jessica had convinced her that he was a really great person. Then, after meeting him and hanging out with him for a while, she believed it. She loved him as a dear friend and trusted him immeasurably.

SHE HAD FIRST MET FENTON when her sister Jessica asked him to pick her up at the Hahnemann University Hospital in Philadelphia, Pennsylvania.

Ironically, it was January 3rd, 1989, exactly two years to the day, that she had been flown by helicopter from South Shore Hospital, near Capetown, to that hospital, where she laid in intensive care for three weeks with a fractured skull, fluid on the brain, and temporary amnesia that lasted for nearly a year following the incident.

She had been living with a boyfriend who was thirteen years her senior named Jesse.

She had met him while dancing at "Down the Hatch" in Capetown. The first Go-Go Bar she ever danced in, in New Jersey.

It had been love at first sight for her. She dated him for a year, before they finally moved in together. They had only been living with each other for about three months, when they had thrown a nice party at their home, on New Years Eve. Ali's parents, who lived three miles away, babysat her two children.

When her mom didn't hear from her for three days, she began to worry.

There was never a day that went by that Ali didn't call to check up on her children. When she didn't return her mother's calls, her mother went over to the house to investigate.

She found her daughter semi-conscious, lying on a couch. Her face was so busted up, that her own mother could hardly recognize her.

Ali's mom immediately helped carry her daughter out to the car and then drove her straight to the nearest hospital. Her younger sister Claire had taken the ride with them. Soon after, she was flown by helicopter to the head trauma center.

Claire had been working as a dispatcher for the Capetown Police Department and told her co-workers, the police, what had happened. Jesse denied the allegations and told them she had gotten drunk and had fallen.

She had been drinking a lot, however, she recalls him grabbing her by the back of her hair in the bedroom, tossing her face into the hard wooden platform of their queen sized waterbed as if he were a big ferocious dog playing with his little rag doll toy. He just kept smashing her against the bed like an angry mad man out of control.

He continued beating her into unconsciousness, while yelling, "get the fuck up you drunk bitch".

She never pressed charges on him because she "loved him" insatiably. She figured he never would have done such a horrible thing to her, if he hadn't been drinking. But Jesse was a manic depressive alcoholic who was not going to stop drinking, and most likely, would have done something much worse to her the next time, so for her own safety, she had to leave him.

Heartbroken.

> Dancing on the stage at night,
> Waiting patiently for Mr. Right.
> Hoping he'll come passing through
> Just to stop to have a few.
> He looks into my big brown eyes
> Suddenly he wants to cry.
> He knows that he's the one for me

Picks me up and carry's me,
Out the door without my pay,
Not one more moment, does he let me stay.
He tells me that his love is true
Looks in my eyes, I love him too
Together we shall drive away
Into the darkness
of another day.

Written by Ali

Ali dancing at Down the Hatch

A hopeless romantic, she never gave up trying to make her relationships work, three children later and still hoping that the next one would be different.

AFTER SHE WAS RELEASED FROM the hospital with temporary amnesia, from the brain swelling, she couldn't remember anything, not even her own name. Her short-term memory was shot.

She moved in with her sister Jessica in Waldwick where things were a fog for a while. She took a break from dancing and began hanging out with Fenton who tried to comfort her broken heart when she could remember that she even had one.

Her two children were staying in Florida for a while with their grandmother during that time.

Eventually she recovered and began dancing at a really classy strip club, "Heartbreakers" in Neptune.

Heartbreakers was one of the top Go-Go bars in New Jersey at the time, and most, if not all the dancers had breast implants, hair extensions and really nice sports cars. Some were even centerfolds for the Hustler Magazine and Penthouse.

Ali wanted to be one of them.

Ali at Heartbreakers 1990

One day while she was at home resting, Fenton showed up out of the blue. He threw a deposit slip on her coffee table that read $75,000.00. She was surprised and happy for him. She said "Wow, Fenton, where did you get that?"

He told her that he had just sold one of his properties that he owned in Canada.

Fenton had been a real estate broker who had made a few bad investments and had been temporarily hurting financially. He was so glad that she was his friend during his down time. That he wanted to do something special for her. He asked her "What do you want for your birthday? You can have anything in the world that you want." She told him, she wanted breast implants. They would be an early birthday present.

She had also been dating a guy named Sam, whom she had met at the Village several months before. Sam had just taken out a business loan and offered to pay for her augmentations as well. But she wanted Fenton to pay for them, because he was her friend, and there were no strings attached.

Fenton took her to get them done in a place somewhere in south Jersey, then, took care of her in his home until she was healed.

He told her, he had been a medic in the Army once, and she even allowed him to remove her stitches, when it came time to take them out.

She trusted him emphatically. He even offered to let Sam come to his home to visit her, while she was recovering and didn't seem jealous of him at all. Sam was twenty-eight years old, closer to her age. Ali dated him for almost a year, but then left him after he got her pregnant and wouldn't marry her. She had gone with her sister to get an abortion. She was really disappointed after that, and realized he wasn't the marrying kind. She decided that she wasn't going to have any more kids without getting married to the father first. But she was against using birth control. I guess she missed those sex education classes in high school. Go figure!

SAM WOUND UP MEETING ANOTHER girl, shortly after their split, and then marrying her, followed by three children later. He had told Ali once that, "you don't marry girls like her." What was that suppose to mean? She couldn't find a guy to marry her when she wasn't a stripper, when she was a stay at home mom. So it couldn't have been her profession.

It wasn't her that had issues with marriage, it was the male species, she thought!

After she got her breasts done, her pay went from a few hundred a day, to ten thousand dollars a month, cash. Within a few months, she was able to buy a new, red 944 Porsche' and save thousands to rent a condo and furnish it nicely.

So much for dating the average guy, after that, they either wanted her as a sex toy or they were just simply too intimidated to be with her on any level.

Or maybe, it was that she thought with all the money she had to spend on herself to maintain her up keep, no one could afford her after that. I guess that's what one would consider a "High Maintenance Woman."

It cost a fortune to keep it up. The tanning beds, makeup, nail salons, hair salons, workout gyms, clothes, accessories and whatever else it took. That alone was a job in itself. Who had time for anything else? Then, to have to actually work and take care of the children, she was completely exhausted!

Ali on stage at Down the Hatch

Chapter 3

It was high time to move out of her sister's house and go on her own. She had established the ultimate independence in September of 1990.

She was finally getting to see the results of all her hard work. She had been working six days a week and pulling a double on Fridays because Friday was the best money-making day of the week in that profession.

She had an agent that did most of her bookings from the very first day she began dancing in New Jersey. The woman's name was Anne and Anne really respected her. Ali was very professional and never gave anyone a hard time about anything. There were days when she would be in bed ready to go to sleep and Anne would call her, telling her she was needed in a club somewhere, that some dancer had left or didn't show up or was too drunk to get back on stage. She always got herself together and went, no matter how tired she was.

She loved being needed, and she never got drunk or did drugs or prostituted with any of the customers. She was always smiling and compassionate to the guys that looked down and depressed because she thought she understood them.

She loved to quote the scriptures and did so every chance she got. She would always say that, "God's light shines it's brightest in the darkness, and that she was an angel doing Gods work in the darkest places around."

But there was a side to her that no one saw. It was her lonely, broken heart. No one could feel her pain. She always laughed and tried to make people happy at work, but deep down inside she longed to find the perfect father for her children. Someone who would love her kids as much as he would love her. Her true soul mate! She spent her entire life searching for "true love".

She even began writing a book of poetry on June 2nd 1988, based on her search for Mr. Right. The name of her book was "Until Tomorrow" and began...Witchy Woman...crystal ball... read my future...tell me all...will I live, or will I die... will my lover say good-bye.

SHE WAS A DREAMER, WHOSE dreams always seemed to turn into nightmares, leaving her with one broken heart after another, and more children to love and support without the help of any of their fathers. She wanted ten children, but was always looking for the perfect man with whom to have them. Imagine that!

ONCE, WHILE SHE WAS DANCING on the stage at Heartbreakers, she noticed a guy sitting alone at the bar folding dollar bills into origami. When she approached him, he handed her his card with a dollar bill folded into a butterfly. The card read "Mindreader." She asked him "Are you a psychic?" he said "Yes."

Then she put out her hand for him to read her palm and said "Ok. If you're so psychic, then where's my Mr. Right?" He pretended to be reading her palm and told her he didn't see anyone in the near future for her. She just sighed and replied, "I don't want to hear that."

He also told her that he was a hypnotist and that he could put her under hypnosis, so she could find him herself. So she agreed for him to do it that very night.

She asked him to follow her home after work, and paid him fifty dollars to put her under hypnosis.

This incident happened shortly after her children had already been taken away from her by the state. Perhaps she was already delusional by then, but it seemed to get even more intense after his visit.

He had her lie down on her sofa, with a candle lit then had

her relax as he spoke to her. She closed her eyes and listened to the sound of his voice as she went back in time. No specific time, just back into her past.

She found herself standing at the front door of a huge white plantation house with pink flowers growing up the side and four very large pillars on the front porch. Her heart began pounding with the anticipation of what might be behind the door.

She was frightened from the suspense, but knew that if she didn't open the door and enter inside, for the rest of her life she would always wonder what was behind that closed door.

So, the curiosity got the best of her that night. She opened the door and entered inside. Suddenly, a very peaceful feeling came over her, a feeling of familiarity, as if she'd been there before and wanted to be there.

She noticed a white piano up against the wall and as she began walking towards it, she began to feel incredibly sad. She looked above the piano and saw his portrait. Then she began to cry, "It's him and he has brown eyes." She saw his face! The same face, she had been searching for, her entire life.

Her heart metaphorically tore open, and all the pain she had been storing inside for what seemed like an eternity, poured out. Repressed emotions? She cried as if something had just happened at that very moment, but it hadn't happened at all. She was still lying on the couch imagining this. It wasn't real! But why did it feel so real to her? Why did he look so familiar?

Then, she went upstairs to the bedroom, where she felt hot and suffocating, she was going to pass out if she didn't get some relief. The hypnotist instructed her to open a window. So she went over to the balcony doors and opened them both, instantly cooling off.

She turned to find a four-post bed and a dresser with a wooden box in the center of it. She opened the box and found a gold crucifix necklace and a wallet. When she opened the wallet, she found a photo of herself with ringlets in her hair.

Her hair was brown, but it was her face that she saw, no one else's.

Then she demanded "I'm taking it!" and she held his crucifix necklace tightly in her hands.

An old man and woman were standing behind her. She left the room and went downstairs into what appeared to be a living room. That's when she noticed a wooden box under the picture window. To her surprise, he was lying in the box, wearing a dark uniform with a strip up the side. Her hypnotist asked her "Where are you now?" It was so strange, how she just stepped out of herself, to see that she was sitting beside him, wearing a white lace cotton dress and six months pregnant with his son. Her name was Elizabeth and the year was 1872.

> As I walked into the room,
> a sadness had come over me.
> And there it stood against the wall
> The piano he once played for me.
> And up above I saw his face
> Then I began to cry,
> As I notice when I got real close
> He had those big brown eyes.
> In his room I found a little box
> And I had to look inside it.
> And when I did, I found a cross
> and a picture of me in his wallet.
> He lie there wearing gold and blue
> and at that moment I finally knew
> that in this life I will find him again
> And when I do, my search will end

Written by Ali

She dreamed of Mr. Right, a man she lost in her past life. But even if she found him now, why would he want her and not someone else? Someone he felt was more pure, someone more innocent. She was a creature of the world now. Too exposed to the harsh realities of life. She was far from being a sheltered woman, used and abused with lots of baggage and psychological disorders from being exposed to the elements.

The eyes are the windows to the soul and when the soul sees all the corruption of the world, it becomes tainted and traumatized.

Love becomes a chemical imbalance that you try to fix but can't. A disorder that you seek therapy for, but find none. An addiction that you try to control, but when it's out of control becomes the most passionate of all feelings.

DSM-IV

Persons with Borderline Personality Disorder are:

"Extremely sensitive to environmental circumstances, Idealizing lovers at first sight, wanting to spend all their time with them. Feeling abandoned when they have to be away from that person.

Having an identity disturbance and an unstable sense of self or a poor self-image.

Going from a needy person to an avenger. Having a self-image that is either good or evil.

No shades of Gray, just black or white.

They may spend money irresponsibly, engage in unsafe sex, binge eat, drive recklessly and have impulsivity problems."

Believe me when I say that every part of the human psyche is in the DSM! So does that mean we're all crazy or have disorders? That's what makes each person in this world uniquely individual. Doesn't it? Does that mean we shouldn't be raising our children if we are diagnosed with a disorder?

That's what it meant for her and her children, who never got to be with their mother again.

ALCOHOL IS A DRUG. A very dangerous drug that impairs your judgment while driving and causes some people to become very abusive and violent, and yet it's legal and there are bars everywhere that sell it. How many people get DUI's, or into car accidents because of it? It should be banned for public use, but since the prohibition, it's society's standard of use. So that makes it OK?

Thank God for the Domestic Violent laws that got passed after the OJ Simpson situation. Now maybe more abused women can be protected from those alcoholic abusers.

Smoking cigarettes is considered a maladaptive behavior, so if a person has a maladaptive behavior, should they be raising children? Smoking cigarettes in a house with a child in there, or in a car with a child breathing in the second hand smoke should be considered child endangerment, shouldn't it? Since second hand smoke is suppose to be so bad for your health. And yet, the only town in New Jersey that has a law against smoking in a car with an infant or child is Key Port. No other place has made it a law. Yet!

They should!

So, if society accepts it as "Normal" then it's fine. But if society decides that it's wrong, then it becomes a law and thus is "against the law to practice?" If you break the law, you get a fine, if you don't pay the fine you get arrested and or sent to jail.

Whatever! You know the routine.

The big problem now with this country is the abuse of prescription drugs. That's societies "Norm" and it's killing thousands of people everyday. But as long as the pharmaceutical companies make their money and share it with the government?

Whatever it may be, when it comes to the authorities, they are very good at taking all those personality traits and turning them against you for their own purpose.

Chapter 4

It took the prosecution nearly two years to create a story that made enough sense to a jury, to indict her. Their story was so well thought out, that even Ali her self, almost believed it. It made complete sense. However, none of it was true. She had to keep telling herself, "Remember the truth!"

"The truth is ...Satan is the father of the lie. He can take one ounce of the truth and twist it so cleverly that it appears to be the entire truth and yet, it is not even close. Completely fascinating! That is how he has managed to deceive practically the entire world." "Out of evil comes good!" Ali's father always said.

Imagine trying to convince a psychologist of this theory. Of course you'll be diagnosed as delusional afterwards. Yet the majority of the world believes that God came down to Earth in the form of a man named Jesus, to save us all from our sins. What a nice guy! Ya see what they did to him?

Ali could feel the incredibly dark powers of the evil she had to face. Beginning with Fenton Noor (The most evil of them all) who worked with the prosecutor telling them he would plead guilty if they prosecuted her too, and then the Judge who was completely on their side working with the prosecution. "Fear none of those things which thou shalt suffer: behold, the Devil shall cast some of you into prison, that ye may be tried. Be thou faithful unto death and ye shall be given the crown of life."- Revelation 2:10. She just couldn't forget what she had once read in a Christian bible.

She had faced the devil many times in her life and knew of his power. This situation was him again in a different guise.

She knew the bible very well. Ever since she was a little girl, her father used to preach to her and began teaching it to her from the very beginnings of her life.

So how was she able to be in a strip club doing what she was doing knowing it was wrong? She justified it, by saying she was only going into Sodom to make money, but she wasn't staying, and she wouldn't partake in the perversions that she saw happening all around her. Drugs, homosexuality, prostitution etc., in her mind, she was an angel doing the work of the Lord by comforting the lost sinners. We are ALL sinners. It was a two edged sword that would eventually turn on her.

Chapter 5

Immediately after the verdict was read, a Sheriff's officer hurried to the table where the young woman stood with her attorney beside her. Handcuffs were placed on her tiny wrists behind her back and she was quickly escorted from the building.

"Do you have any last words Ms. Durant?" A reporter yelled out just before she was taken away. The twenty eight year old woman who had never before been in this kind of trouble, frozen from the shock of the situation, blurted out the only words her mind could think of at that moment. "He was a cleaver man! He set me up!" She wanted to say more, but her mouth wouldn't open. Her brain went into a fog. Too weak to even look for her mother and her best friend, Marc Sky. They had been there all week to give their moral support. She didn't even get the chance to say good-bye to them or thank them for being there for her.

It was a very cold winter day and she was rushed out of the room so quickly that it was forgotten to put on her long, warm, hunter green wool coat. How could she anyway with her hands bound? She didn't even think about it. Not even when she was assisted into the white van that would take her from the courthouse to the county jail where she would await sentencing for seven months. Her body shivered uncontrollably on the freezing metal bench inside the vehicle.

Suspended in time, everything seemed surreal now, like a bad dream that was happening too quickly or a death without actually dying. For the first time in her entire life she felt the difference between her body and her soul. Her soul longed to be free, but was now trapped in the physical body that no longer belonged to her. It belonged to the State and she had no control as to where they would take it.

It seemed like an eternity that she would freeze in this long drive without anything to warm her. Then, suddenly, without warning, the van stopped and the back door opened. "Please step out of the vehicle!" said a voice, as several officers assisted her. She didn't speak a word, not a sound. She just went with them into what would become a living HELL. Only this hell was not with burning fire, it was with bitter cold, colder than she had ever recalled feeling.

She thought to herself "I'm dead now and if I don't talk, I'll stay dead. Talking will mean that my body is reconnected to my soul and then I won't be dead. I have to keep quiet for as long as this nightmare exists."

She traveled up an elevator with her uniformed escort and was brought into a big yellow room called "A holding Cell". With dingy yellow and gray cinderblock walls and only a metal cot with a tattered, old, ugly, faded, light blue mattress and stainless steal toilet/sink combo.

A very nice older lady with big frosted blonde hair in a sheriff's officer's uniform and bright pink lipstick, came into the room with two paper gowns to put on the prisoner who just stood still as if waiting to see what happened next. The officer's name was Dee. She smelled of cigarette smoke and had a raspy smokers voice. Dee helped the woman in shock remove all of her clothing.

First, her glasses that helped her see the injustice being done to her. Second, her taupe colored low heal shoes, then the conservative dress, white stockings and a crucifix from around her neck. Both of her earrings and the gold rings on her fingers were removed as well. She couldn't even wear her watch.

Everything was taken away from her, even the rubber band that held her French braid in her hair. A paper gown was put on her front-side and one was put on her back to cover her backside. And then Dee left the brightly lit room, closing the door behind her as the door automatically locked itself.

She was alone now with only the silence to keep her company and the bitter cold. It was still exceptionally freezing in that almost empty cell. There wasn't a pillow or a blanket, not even a sheet to cover the dirty, germ ridden, two-inch thick mattress that laid across the metal cot, which bolted to the floor. The paper gowns were a security measure for those on suicide watch. They supposed, that if a person, wanted to kill themselves, they could use just about anything to do it. And desperate people can be very creative.

But she didn't need to be. In her mind THEY already killed her. The only thing they didn't do, was bury the body. They kept it in a freezer awaiting transport. So her soul was forced to wait for hours in a shivering human body that didn't belong to her any longer.

Sitting on the edge of the bed, she just sat there in a state of shock. Trying to absorb the past week, no, the past few years. Taking it one second at a time and one breath at a time. She was still breathing. Wondering why she hadn't passed over into the afterlife. She was sure her life was over. The gypsy's crystal ball had turned black. She saw it herself. No future, just death.

She had faced the most humiliating accusations a human being could face, especially a caring, loving mother. She thought to her self, "I am dead to anyone who ever knew me. How could I ever face anyone again? My career is over, my reputation destroyed, and the hardest thing to face, is the fact that I have lost my beautiful children forever. I will never again get to tuck them into bed and read them bedtime stories. I can only pray now that the God in Heaven looks over them, protecting them and keeping them safe, healthy and happy. And I am so sorry my children for failing you." she thought

"I don't deserve to live. A mother who fails to protect her children is worthless. And worse than that, the whole world now believes that I did it intentionally for my own personal gratifications.

They are so wrong! I didn't know until it was too late and the damage was already done. I trusted him. I never in a million years thought that he would do something like that, especially to my children. I thought he loved me. I believed him when he told me he would keep them safe. I was so stupid! How could I have trusted a man to watch my children? Men are fucked up. When will I ever learn? I deserve everything that God allows to happen to me," she thought to herself.

"I know exactly why this happened and how this happened. It's because I had sex with a married man and caused him to commit adultery. I knew better and still broke one of the most sacred of the commandments. We can all justify our behavior to suit our own desires, but wrong is wrong and there are always consequences no matter who we are."

Chapter 6

Years before, when she was still pregnant with her youngest son Tyler and living with Adam Sr., Adam was not being a responsible father, nor was he being a good mate. He was gone all week from 6 AM to 10 PM working as a Sub-contractor for a building company. He reminded her of Jesus, the Jewish carpenter. Only he was six foot two, two hundred and forty pounds of pure muscle, and the strong silent type, without a doubt. He had been a professional kick boxer and had a third degree black belt. The epitome of big, bad and ugly she always said. And he loved smoking weed!

Adam had been spending all of his time in the strip clubs while he was supposed to be working, and instead of buying food and diapers for his child at home, he would buy cocaine and marijuana and party with the strippers. So Ali was forced to go on welfare and get food stamps to survive. They lived in a house that was heated with oil and instead of buying oil to heat the house, Adam would come home with wood from his construction jobs and burn it in the small wood burning stove in the den. That didn't last long, than the house would be freezing again.

The only other source she had, to heat the house in the winter, was a small electric heater that her father had given her. She kept it on in the bedroom at night with the door closed. Both of her children would sleep in her bed with her to keep warm. The seat cover on the toilet in the bathroom was as cold as an ice cube.

Adam was making truck payments to a used car dealer on Route 19 in Waldwick. His name was Joey. He was the owner of J&R Auto. Adam had missed some payments, so Joey repossessed his vehicle.

Ali's dad knew Joey well, and she always felt the need to help Adam, so she decided to go to the lot one day with her father to try to convince Joey to give Adam back his truck so he could work. Joey was very understanding of her situation knowing she was six months pregnant with two other children to care for.

She told him she didn't have oil to heat her house because Adam wouldn't provide for his family. Joey, who couldn't understand why such a beautiful girl could be with such a guy, out of the kindness of his heart, reached into his pocket and pulled out sixty dollars. He handed it to her and told her to go get some heat in her house. Ali was only nineteen years old at the time and was so impressionable and grateful for his charity, that she told him she would pay him back someday. She didn't know when, but she would.

Adam convinced her when Tyler was a few months old to move to Jacksonville, Florida with him and he wound up abandoning her down there after only a few months. Well, the truth was, after trying to make their relationship work for four years, she just got tired of his bullshit. All they ever did was fight about his lack of responsibility and his partying. She couldn't take it anymore, so she asked him to leave one morning and he did. Ali thought that she would be happy in a paradise with palm trees and beautiful beaches, but she wasn't. And she knew why. She was with the wrong guy. He never even attempted to give her another dime after he left to help her with the children, two of which were still in diapers and his.

Two weeks after Adam left her, he met a barmaid at a bar called the "Tide" on Jax beach. It was a biker bar and his girlfriend was a tall, masculine looking, German girl named Sasha. Ali had met her a few times and let her know that she had absolutely nothing to be jealous of. She didn't love Adam enough, to want him any longer.

Ali was left all alone in an unfamiliar place to survive with her three children. Tyler was only nine months old at the time.

Her parents could only afford to send her twenty-five dollars a week, which wasn't enough to provide anything except some bologna and cheese, some bread and juice. Not even diapers. She had to find a job or her children would starve. Welfare was fifty miles away and she had no vehicle to get her there.

SHE HAD BEEN STAYING IN a fairly large trailer park right outside of the May Port Navy Base. Most of the people living in the park were military Navy people and their families. She had met some of the other mothers while pushing her baby stroller around the park searching for diapers. She would ask anyone passing by with a baby in a stroller, if they could spare a few diapers for her children. She never had enough money to buy her own. Everyone seemed so nice there and no one ever turned her down. Most of the women spent months alone raising their children, while their husbands were away at sea. And they longed for conversation and friendship as much as Ali did. She tried so hard to stay strong for her children, but it was a very challenging situation.

There was no electricity in the trailer and no locks on the doors to make her feel safe at night. And her trailer was loaded with cockroaches. She had to keep food and drinks in a cooler and at night light candles to see. She cried herself to sleep almost every night wishing someone would come rescue her and make her happy again. But no one ever did and she had to learn to become independent.

THERE WAS ONLY ONE BAR right outside the Navy base called "Jerry's North". It was also right down the street, walking distance from the trailer park, exactly one mile from her trailer that she would never call home, because to her it never was. There was nothing else around for miles except a laundry mat with a pay phone where Ali could call home once in a while to talk to her family.

Then one day she finally decided it was about time to ask them for help. She was extremely desperate by then and frightened that her children would wind up dying from malnutrition. The reality was, she just couldn't do it any longer by her self. She realized she loved Adam with all her heart, but knew it was time to grow up and be a woman. She was twenty-one years old and had spent most of her teen years tied down in dysfunctional relationships. She lived threw the identity of her emotionally abusive, sometimes physically abusive mates, who did things she was so against, opposites attracting to each other?

She tried to be a good girl. She studied the bible and did her best to provide for her children. But she had failed to provide the most important aspect to completing the perfect family. The family she felt God had intended for all human beings to have. She failed to provide a descent father for her children. Although Adam never hurt her in an unforgiving way and would remain her friend forever, they never again would be together as boyfriend and girlfriend or become husband and wife.

Right before he had walked out of her life, she told him out of anger that "Someday she would be on the receiving end of the dollar bills that he had been giving to all those sexy girls with the pretty faces and nice ass's." And subconsciously that's exactly what she set out to do.

She found out that Adam's mother was about to take a trip to Alabama to visit Adam's sister Kathy and asked her if she would come and pick up Amanda to bring back to New Jersey to her parents. Ali's parents loved Amanda and wanted her with them. Adam's mother loved little Adam and wanted him with her. So, Ali agreed to give Adam's mother little Adam if she came and took Amanda with her. Little Adam who Ali nicknamed "Bogey" was only two years old and had never even spent a single night away from his mother. Amanda practically grew up with Ali's parents, so it wasn't as hard to let her go.

The reality didn't hit until the day Adam's mom showed up at her door to take the kids back to New Jersey with her. It was the hardest thing Ali had ever had to do in her life up to that point. She had to let her children go, knowing she couldn't take care of them. She had failed! She failed as a woman to satisfy the desires of her men, and she failed as a mother to take care of her children. She loved them with ALL of her heart, but to keep them safe and healthy she had to say good-bye to them and let them go.

Adam Jr. cried and held onto his mother's neck so tight that he was choking her. He begged her not to make him go. Her heart broke into a billion pieces that day. She just wanted to die.

But with only a nine month old to care for, it was a lot easier to get a babysitter. She found a woman in the park that had a slew of her own kids, but especially loved babies. So she left Tyler with her and went to find a job. The first place she went to was Jerry's North. She asked them if they needed a bartender, I mean how hard can it be to serve beer? But they said they only needed dancers, topless Go-Go dancers. So that night, with only one light blue negligee she had just purchased from a K-Mart down town, she began what would soon become her career. As it would happen though, she only had to get up on the stage twice without her top on, because at midnight that very night, the laws changed, and there were no more topless bars allowed in that county. She truly felt that God was looking out for her that night when it happened.

Chaotic Paradise

It was so very humiliating for her at first to get up on stage and dance. She felt like she had just walked into the city of Sodom with all the perverts staring up at her. And she knew nothing about exotic dancing. But after she drank some alcohol and watched the other girls, who enjoyed teaching her the ropes, she eventually got the hang of it. She made friends with the dancers and DJ and made some money. It wasn't the ideal job, but what was a young girl with zero experience and a child to take care of supposed to do? The bar people became her family and Jerry the owner was the father who protected all the girls. He was actually gay so none of the girls ever had to worry about him taking advantage of them.

Ali knew how to shoot pool, so she got herself a pool stick and began hustling the drunk, sailors out of their pay, beating them more often then not. She actually made more money at the pool tables, than she did table dancing for the customers. She wasn't really into the dancing thing anyway and if she could spend the day on the tables, it was way more fun for her.

She felt like a kid in the candy store with all the attention she was getting from the variety of men. So many of them, most of them around twenty-four years old and extremely attractive, sexy, single, lonely sailors with lots of money to spend when they came back into port.

She especially loved them in their sailor uniforms. One at a time Ali began exploring their worlds. She was finally having fun and hanging out every night with the friends she met at the bar. They would all go out after work to a dance club called "Captain Odies," where she began drinking herself into oblivion.

The guilt consumed her, of her failures as a mother and she partied hard almost everyday to forget it. She hated being sober. She even took some pills one night while drinking and wound up nearly dying. The person, who found her, said she had stopped breathing. That he had to beat on her chest to revive her. She didn't remember anything. She was sowing her oats and wallowing in self-pity at the same time.

Eventually, she had awakened one morning in someone else's bed. Naked! Someone, whom she had seen countless times before in the bars, but was not in the least bit interested in. Ali told him that because of him, she was finally going back home. She had had enough! She was going back home to try to piece her life together so she could be with her children again.

She missed them a lot! God wouldn't let her die, so she had to try to live. And this wasn't the life she really wanted for herself. It was a great vacation with palm tree's and Pina Coladas, but all good things must come to an end.

Ali went back to her hotel room where she had been staying after moving out of the trailer, and called her mother who had been waiting for that final phone call. She told her mother that she had had enough and was coming home. Her mother yelled "Hooray!! Finally she comes to her senses!" Ali thanked the woman who had been taking good care of her son and paid her well. Then she packed up her things and gathered Tyler.

SHE HAD FOUND AN ADORABLE Spanish guy in the bar to take her back to New Jersey. His family lived in Spanish Harlem, New York. She had been dating him for a few months. His name was Fernando Lopez. He was a sheet rocker with long, beautiful, curly black hair and eyes so dark you couldn't even see his pupils. He was built like an Adonis and Ali wanted to show him off to her family. So they headed North with Tyler, in Fernando's old, beat up tan jalopy.

It was around 1987 or 88, during the time when the cops were after drug smugglers. Fernando's car got stopped in almost every state traveling north on Interstate 95 to get searched. The police had even made her take Tyler out of the car once, so they could pull the back seat down to search behind it. I guess they had fit the profile of the people who could be smuggling drugs. Thank God Fernando wasn't one of them or I'd be telling a different story about Ali now.

By the time they got to New Jersey, they had been stopped so many times that she was so tired of it all. When the last state trooper finally stopped them in New Jersey, Ali asked him if he would please write a note saying that their car had already been searched. She just wanted to get back home to her parents and her other children. What an event!

When she finally got to her parents and brought Fernando inside to meet everyone, her dad began freaking out screaming! "Get that fucking cockroach out of my house!"

"Oh my God!" He was prejudice against his daughter being with a Spanish guy. Who would have guessed? He told her that she should stay with her own race of people. Ali always believed that God created all men equal so why should it matter what the culture was? To be honest, her father never thought that any man was good enough for his daughter and just used that as an excuse. So she had to say good-bye to Fernando. He wasn't welcomed there. But not before she went with him to his home in Spanish Harlem. I don't think it went so well for him either, being with her and a baby. All she remembers is Fernando's mother yelling at him something in Spanish that he told her later meant, "Go to hell or seek the devil!"

THE GREAT ADVENTURE WAS OVER!

Ali was finally safe at home with her family, now living in Capetown, New Jersey. A big change from the area she had just come from. Flannel shirts and fisherman were her perception of that place. She had found "Down The Hatch" and her agent Anne and within two weeks she had steady employment as a Go-Go dancer in New Jersey. So much for getting away from that lifestyle, it had followed her home.

Tsunami

Chapter 7

Anne was a great agent who worked with all the bars in New Jersey and got her another gig at "Millers" in Federton, which was a little south of Capetown.

Ali knew that she couldn't run around with a lot of guys there or she'd get a bad reputation quickly. She didn't want anyone to think she was a whore, even though she was a dancer. So, she waited for Mr. Right to come into the bar and take her breath away.

It only took three weeks before she found Jesse at the Hatch with his friend Tim. He was thirty-six years old and drove a brand new, silver Jaguar. He worked at "Mettina's Bread World" in Wareton, the next town north of Capetown. He was very impressive to the twenty-four year old. It was love at first sight for her and she spent every chance she could trying to make him fit into her idea of the perfect father figure for not only herself, but her children as well. He had an eight-year old son and had been divorced for a while. He was an ex-musician who played guitar and sang. Ali loved musicians! She had made up her mind that her Mr. Right had to have these five qualities to be with her. Long, dark wavy hair, green or blue eyes, a nice car, be a musician and a great kisser/lover. A father to her children would have to come later. Jesse fit the profile to a T!

She used to dance until 1 AM then go to his job where he worked from 6 PM to 6 AM baking bread. She would hang out with him all night sometimes while her parents babysat. Then on days when neither of them were working, they would either take the kids to the Seaside boardwalk or Jesse would hang out with her alone in a bar drinking and serenading her with the acoustic guitar she had bought for him, intended for just that.

And then, about six months after they began seeing each other, she crashed her car into a tree one night at Down the Hatch, when she was drunk. She had been driving to see him in the rain.

She shattered her right clavicle and wound up in the hospital for a week. During her hospital stay, Jesse had gotten drunk at the Hatch and wound up sleeping with the barmaid. A short, over weight forty-year old woman who couldn't hold a candle to her.

SHE FORGAVE HER CHEATING LOVER, justifying it, that he had to have been drunk to be with her friend Linda. Linda was actually the one who gave her the details of that night, after Ali told her that Jesse had confessed to it. Ali tricked her into telling her the truth. She was always very perceptive when it came to people. Or so she thought! She was also very confident in herself by then and wasn't intimidated by other women. That's why she had invited Linda and her newly found beau to her New Years Eve party.

She had just given Jesse a seven hundred and fifty dollar gunmetal blue, fender Stratocaster for Christmas a few days earlier, and Jesse had the audacity to be flirting with someone right in her face after knowing that he slept with that hussy. Ali got really jealous and began drinking Cold Duck by the bottle. She called him an asshole in front of everyone because he had been bragging to them all about his accomplishments, the house on the water, the beautiful furniture and everything else, when it was all she who had done it. She was the one who rented them the house. She was even making his car payments. And Jesse had become some insecure, neurotic, control freak, thinking that every time she went to work, she was cheating on him. As it is said "The guilty will accuse". After the party was over Ali was so drunk that she was on the floor, on all fours in the bedroom and couldn't get up. That's when Jesse came in behind her and grabbed her by the back of the head nearly killing her. She left Capetown to live with her sister Jessica after that and was never with him again.

Ali never lived with another guy after that either. Her brother Chris and Adam Sr. were going to fuck Jesse up for doing that to "Adam's child's mother", but she begged them not to. She still loved him with all her heart and figured God would punish him in due time.

Jesse eventually lost his job, his Jaguar and his good looks. He got bloated from the alcohol and looked like he was under a curse the next time she saw him a year later. Oh yeah, the reason he lost his job, was because he had been screwing his boss's seventeen-year old daughter, Beth.

For some reason, after everyone in town found out about the young girl being with him, they stopped believing his story and began believing Ali, that he had hurt her intentionally. Before that, Ali had no credibility with her story. Everyone thought Jesse had told the truth that she had fallen. I don't know why? Did she look like a liar to everyone? What's a liar look like anyway?

Chapter 8

Ali had recovered from the assault on her body and soul once again and was now dancing at the Village in Waldwick. She had gotten her breast implants from Fenton and had finally moved out of her sisters into her own Condo in Brandon, New Jersey on Brandy Ave.

She had broken up with her boyfriend Sam and was looking better and feeling better than she ever did. She had very high self-esteem and was very proud of her accomplishments. She now owned her own red 944 Porsche and decided it was high time that she paid back the used car dealer Joey, for his unconditional kindness when she was an immature, insecure, dependent, loser. So she went to his car lot, but Joey wasn't there at that time, so she left her calling card.

She had the guys, who were working lay a blanket down on the floor of the garage, and she danced for them in a seductive costume. They had paid her well for her performance. One of the guys just happened to be Joey's cousin, who couldn't wait to tell Joey all about it.

Sure enough, within a week, Joey came waltzing thru the doors of the Village looking for her, she just happened to be up on stage at the time. Joey was looking better than ever and couldn't believe how Ali had grown into such a beautiful young woman. For her, it was just great to see him again. She wanted to show off her independence. No more loser guys dragging her down. Her children had a female babysitter when Fenton wasn't watching them, and they all wore designer clothes, ate in the best restaurants and went to zoos, museums and parks when she wasn't working.

She knew that Joey had been married for sixteen years and had two children of his own. Both were still in diapers at the time, but she just loved hanging out with him. He was a very sexy Italian Man who owned his own business where everyone looked up to him like he was the Godfather of used cars. She also knew that she had a special bond with him that was more than just a man and a woman or stripper and customer; he was like family to her.

He knew Ali's father and mother and they loved him. Her mom thought he was so handsome. I'm sure if she could have, she would have been with him herself. But as much as Ali adored him, he was still married and she was superstitious about having sex with a married man.

After hanging out with him for a few months and having him spoil her with all sorts of gifts, including a brand new four thousand dollar, queen sized, canopy water bed, and then bringing over a Christmas tree with all the trimmings and spending a fortune on her kids, including buying them a new puppy Chihuahua for Christmas, she didn't know what to give a guy who had everything already. So she asked him what he wanted and he said "I want you to make love to me." She thought long and hard about it knowing it was wrong to do. But decided that she would, only it would have to be after the holidays. He would spend Christmas with his family and New Years, then on January 3rd 1991, she would make arrangements with a babysitter to watch her kids over night, so they wouldn't be in the house with her while she was having sex with a man.

She never wanted her kids to see her waking up in bed with a man that wasn't their father. She was weird that way. She also didn't want to be interrupted in the throws of passion, with one of them walking in on her either.

So, when the time came, she asked Fenton if he would watch her two children so she could sleep with Joey. Fenton got angry or just jealous and said, "You'll be with a married man, but you won't be with me". She tried to convince him that they were best of friends and that if she slept with him, she would never look at him the same way again and that she would most likely hate him for it.

So, he told her he would watch Amanda, but not Tyler. He argued that Tyler was a brat. To be honest, Tyler was a brat. But he was a very cute one and Ali didn't want Fenton to do anything to hurt him out of anger, so she got Tyler a different babysitter for that night.

A few days before that fateful night, she was in her shower washing her hair when she asked the "Spirits" if it was Ok if she had sex with Joey. She said "If God is a God of love and I'm doing this out of love, is it wrong?" The water just stopped flowing while her hair was still full of lather. "Ok, I guess that means No?" The water automatically turned back on. She said "Just once?" and the water cut off again. "Ok I won't!" and the water turned back on. She figured that it was a sign from God not to have sex with him. She knew that if the spirits could turn her water off like that, they could burn her house down or kill her children or anything, so she decided not to. She thought that she would be too scared to defy God. How was she going to be able to disappoint the man who had shown her more kindness than anyone had ever shone in her entire life, other than her parents?

Stupid, Stupid Girl!!! I guess that's the "Free Will" that's spoken of in the bible. But it's not like she was a virgin or anything. She certainly wasn't Mother Teresa. So why would it even matter? She thought.

Of course she went against her own better judgment and when the time came, she lit some candles on her dresser and the candles began burning sporadically with flames shooting high and then going out. Another sign! Then... Joey couldn't get hard. He said he had never been with another woman since he got married. Another sign! She was freaking out and hoping to get out of it all. But then, he managed to get on top of her thin, tanned, naked body and stick himself inside of her. She was cringing with fear and disgust at herself. He was not her type and she was not enjoying this one bit. It was a HUGE mistake that she was making.

He began humping away like a dog in heat, panting and groaning and sweating from head to toe. The sweat was just poring off of him. It had covered his entire forehead. While she was staring up at him in desperation for it to be over, she suddenly felt a drop of his nasty bodily fluid, fall directly into her opened eye, instantly burning it like acid. She screamed from the pain, which exited him into ejaculate. He grunted like a big hairy dog that just exploded his load into this foolish idiot of a woman.

And then, instead of climbing off of her and going into the shower to wash off the sex sweat, he rolled over onto her crisp, clean new sheets. How disgusting! She thought. She would NEVER do this again, no matter what.

THE NEXT MORNING, SHE WOKE to a phone call from her daughter Amanda. It was exactly 7:20 Am. She had looked at the clock next to her bed as soon as she opened her eyes. Her daughter was still at Fenton's house in Brandon where she had often spent so many nights before in the past few months. She told her mother that Fenton had molested her. That he kept trying to kiss her but she cracked him in the face with her elbow. Then she told her mother that Fenton had pulled his pee-pee out and made white stuff come out of it. She said that he didn't hurt her or put his penis in her, but he had licked her private part.

Ali told her daughter to put Fenton on the phone and then asked him if what Amanda was saying was true. He denied it and said, she was just saying that, because he wouldn't give her ice cream for breakfast.

She knew that her daughter couldn't make up a story like that. She was only seven years old and wouldn't know anything about white stuff coming out of a penis unless she actually saw it.

She jumped up out of bed in a panic and began pacing the floor in her bedroom not knowing what to do next. She immediately felt her daughter was in grave danger. She thought that a man, who was capable of molesting a child, was also capable of killing one too. Amanda was eight miles away and if Ali freaked out in panic, there was no telling what this guy would have done.

She imagined that he would take her daughter deep into a wooded area and kill her so she wouldn't be able to tell on him.

Ali, who suffered from post-traumatic stress disorder, was most likely having a flashback at that moment, of her experience when she was sixteen years old, when her husband on her wedding night threatened to kill her and put her body into the woods where no one would be able to find it. A situation she would remember forever and link to anyone who was, in her perception, insane.

She took a deep breath and tried to remain calm for her daughter's sake. She didn't want her daughter to be victimized again by this maniac, so she told him that she didn't believe her daughter and that he should just take her to her school bus like he always did, so she could go to school.

That was the routine when Amanda stayed at his house over night. She felt that if she continued the routine as usual, he wouldn't be alarmed, panic and react. Desperate people do desperate things!

She asked Fenton to put Amanda back on the phone. When she got on the phone, her mother said, "Amanda, mommy believes you, but you are in great danger with this guy, so you don't want to alarm him in anyway or he will hurt you. Stay calm and act like I don't believe you, so he will take you to your bus stop. When you get to your bus stop, tell him that you need to use the bathroom at Peggy's house (Her other babysitter, who had watched Tyler the night before). When you get into Peggy's house tell her everything you just told me and have her call me immediately to let me know that you are safe. DO NOT go back outside to Fenton. Wait there until I come and get you. Do you understand?" Amanda said she understood and did exactly what her mother told her to do. She was a very bright child and her mother knew this.

She paced the floor for what seemed like an eternity until she got that call from Peggy. When she knew that her daughter was safe from Fenton, she told Peggy not to call the authorities until she got there.

No one touches her children without regret, she thought to herself. She would make sure that Adam Sr. knew what had happened so they could both, without question take care of that piece of shit pedophile!

There were no cell phones back then, only pagers. And Ali tried paging Adam for what seemed like hours with no reply. Where the hell was he when she needed him more then she ever needed him before?

She got another idea. She was booked for the Village that day so she would go in as usual and discreetly wait for her biker friends who would definitely make sure that Fenton never touched another child for the rest of his life, which she hoped would be expiring shortly.

But what a stupid idea that was! Would you believe of all the days for them NOT to be there, it was that one particular day. How could that be, she thought, they were always there. The manager Eddie was very good friends with them all, and they always hung out there. Now what would she do?

She had no idea what was actually going on behind her back at the prosecutor's office. It looked so bad for her in the end.

But fuck the courts, she thought! What would they do? Put him in a jail cell and feed him, clothe him and take care of him until he was let out to do it again to some other child. No way! She was going to have the satisfaction of fucking this guy up her self. Fate! Destiny! Karma!

The timing was way off for revenge. By the time Ali got a hold of Adam Sr., Peggy had already called the authorities, and had taken the two children to the prosecutor's office.

Ali got a call at the Village that her kids were at the prosecutor's office in downtown Waldwick.

Ok. So she couldn't find anyone to take care of Fenton. Peggy said that Fenton had come back and knew that the police were looking for him. So he took off and hid at his daughter's house for a few days until he turned himself into the authorities. He knew that Ali had finally informed Adam and some of her biker friends about him and that they were also looking for him. Ali's sister, Jessica, had informed Fenton of the posse searching for him. So he felt that he would be much safer with the police than if her friends had found him, and he turned himself into the authorities.

What a nightmare it was turning out to be for her. The first thing that looked bad was the fact that she didn't call the police as soon as she found out about the sexual assault on her daughter. The second thing was that her daughter kept talking about bags of money that mommy always had lying around the house. The authorities assumed that Fenton had been paying her money to be with her daughter.

That was so insanely absurd! I mean, if she had gotten any money from anyone it was Joey and certainly not Fenton. But the truth was that she was making for herself about ten thousand dollars a month, cash at the bars and didn't use a bank to leave a paper trail. Fenton was just a babysitter who got paid very poorly by Ali, since she figured that he really didn't need her money. He had plenty of his own.

Ok, so she was a little spoiled with guys giving her cash, but she wasn't crazy enough to rent her daughter out to some pedophile for it. Fenton and Joey both helped her once with some repairs she had to make on her Porsche. The authorities used everything that Fenton did to help Ali out as her excuse for exploiting her daughter.

She had never even thought that someone was capable of such heinous acts. But the authorities didn't put anything past anyone. Wow! They must have seen some crazy shit in their day to think that someone could actually do something like that.

It's absolutely insane! And after they spoke with her daughter, that's exactly what they thought she was. Completely insane!

When she got to the prosecutor's office, she told her daughter to tell them the truth, and Amanda looked up at her mother with such a defiant attitude and said "Why? You pay more attention to Tyler than you do me." "Amanda this is no time to be getting even with me about Tyler. Now tell these people the truth!" Amanda just said flat out "NO!" So Ali looked at her child like she wanted to smack her senseless, but simply said to her, "I'm going to beat your butt when you turn eighteen years old".

The people in the office immediately yelled, "Take the kids!" And that was the end of their meeting. Then they put it in the News Papers that she had threatened to hurt her daughter when she grew up.

What assholes! She thought

They refused to give her children back to her and she couldn't understand why because she hadn't done anything for that to be warranted, in her mind.

She called someone she knew was an attorney, he had given her his card at the Village one day, so she already had his number. Larry showed up at family court several times with her over the next year, but nothing was really said or done.

About five days after Ali's kids were taken from her, she got a strange phone call from Fenton Noor's daughter Tracy, who demanded that Ali Bail her father out of jail for five thousand dollars. She told Ali that she had a "stack of checks" from her father that he had been paying to Ali and said that if Ali didn't bail Fenton out, she was going to turn them over to the police.

Ali knew absolutely nothing about any checks and told her that. She was more concerned about getting all of her children's designer clothes. They had cost her a small fortune and were still in his house. She was hoping to get them back with his daughters help now that she had called.

Ali asked Tracy, "How many checks are there, and how much are they for?" But his daughter didn't know and just said they were at his house.

Ali figured that his daughter must have been the one to cash them if there really were any, because she was his daughter and he needed a girl to cash them. She figured that Fenton was trying to set her up. But she wasn't as concerned about all that. She just wanted the kids clothing and didn't want to hear about all the other drama. It was too much for her brain to consume. She just wasn't into mystery, thrillers! She was more into romantic comedies. This was turning out to be too complicated.

So Ali thought if she appeased this extorting bitch that she would just leave her alone and go away. She told Tracy that she wouldn't say anything to the authorities about her father and told her that she would even call her daughter a liar if anyone asked. Ali also said that she would keep her mouth shut about the molestation and that the authorities wouldn't believe Amanda anyway. But Ali wasn't really going to do that because she wanted to keep that pedophile in jail. Ali thought that Fenton's own daughter and his grand daughter must have been a victim to his sick perversions as well.

Little did Ali know, Fenton's daughter was actually calling her from the prosecutors office while they were taping her conversation, trying to trap her into admitting she had been extorting money from Fenton for molesting her daughter.

This entire situation was too much for her to deal with. They're all out of their fucking minds she thought. Everyone's been playing cops and robbers way too long to think all this stupid bullshit.

Fenton molested Amanda, that one night, and that was it. As far as she knew, it had only happened that one night and it was most likely because Fenton got jealous of Joey. But as the detectives wrote the story, it became far more complicated than that.

Trust No Man! Dedicated to Fenton Noor!

In a world of lies, lust and deception
I fell prey to a man
Heading in the wrong direction.
With our friendship we reached a
Serious understanding that no matter what he does
My children would have his full protection.

Live and let live
But learn to forgive.
I did what I had to do
because I needed to believe in you.
But you chose to let me down
By tainting my child's mind.
So now it's in Gods hands
Know he's not going to be so kind.

Justice does prevail in the end.
Your rein is up. You're no longer my friend.
Your sick, demented, twisted show
Is over now, its time for you to go.

By Ali

Kemgoz

Now lets talk about Ali's state of mind at that time.

The day that her children were taken from her, she collapsed at her home on a couch and couldn't get up. She had been working six days a week, pulling a double on Fridays trying to make as much money as she could, so she could give her children everything that their hearts desired.

Why? Because she was trying to play super Mom, since she

had failed to provide a father for her children, she would try to make up for it in other ways. She had become unintentionally bulimic when she ate and was living off of the caffeine she got from drinking endless amounts of coffee to stay energetic for dancing.

She had collapsed at the bar Body language and was taken to the hospital where the doctor told her she was suffering from malnutrition, dehydration and exhaustion.

She thought that taking two days off from work would be enough, but when she tried to go back to work, she collapsed again. She just couldn't do it any longer.

Her heart was once again broken. They had taken away her only inspiration for success, the reason for her to even be alive. They took away her little boy Tyler, who Ali admits was her pride and joy! She got herself a keyboard and decided to write a song. But these are the words that came out of her. They were actually written to Adam about Adam Jr. She never even realized until that day, how much she was affected by losing her other baby boy years before, to his grandmother who she knew was giving him the more stable life that he needed. She loved all of her children more than life itself, and really just wanted to die, because once again, she had failed them.

> "When you came to me one morning and you said to
> me good-bye,
> How I wanted you to hold me, to wipe the teardrops
> from my eyes.
> But I knew that it was over, we're a love not meant to
> be
> and when I closed the door, in the silence
> I kept a part of you with me.
>
> Why'd you ever leave me all alone, when you knew I
> couldn't make it on my own
> Now your gone, and he's gone and I'm alone.
>
> You see I had a little baby and I named him after you

but I never got to know him and all the things that he
went through
cause one cold and lonely evening as I held him in my
arms
I knew I could never keep him
I'd never do it on my own.

Now my world's so full of sorrow and my love put on
display
and I dream about tomorrow to get me through
another day
and my house is always empty, but I'm never all alone
cause in the echoes of the silence, I never thought that
you'de be gone
Why'd you ever leave me all alone, when you knew I
couldn't make it on my own
Now your gone and he's gone and I'm alone."

After she wrote his song, she gave her keyboard to her son
Adam Jr. and never played it again.

She thought about the day she had finally made it as a top
dancer at "Heartbreakers".

She had been on the stage dancing one night as usual, when
Adam Sr. came in and sat at the bar to watch her. It was a nice
surprise! He had never seen her dance before, until that night.
When she finally finished her set, he tipped her thirty-five
dollars and her heart just broke into a billion pieces.

At that very moment, she had realized that she had finally
achieved her goal. She had climbed to the top of the ladder of
her profession just to get even with him for putting her through
all that he had put her through.

She had loved him in a way that was stronger than any
other guy she had ever been with and for some reason she still
respected him so much.

She wasn't happy with who she had become. She loved
being the wife that stayed at home and took care of the children
while her man worked to provide for his family. She loved

going to church and praying to God for all of her blessings and her beautiful, healthy family. She had stopped doing all those things when she had to work in a strip club. She was ashamed to go into the house of God, knowing she was being ungodly, so she always had an excuse not to find the time.

SHE JUMPED OFF THE STAGE and ran into the dressing room hysterically crying. The other girls went over to her, putting their arms around her, to comfort her, asking what had happened. All she would say was "He tipped me thirty-five dollars". They laughed and said, "Well that's a good thing isn't it?" But to her, it was the end of the long road she had been traveling where she no longer respected the role of the wife, but respected the role of the mistress who got all the perks and none of the headaches. Being the mistress meant being in love with the idea of love, without actually having the love. Does that make any sense? But did the wife get the love? She didn't think so.

Thank God for Joey! Even though she was too depressed to make love to him again, he stood by her side. He went with her every Wednesday so she could visit her children in a supervised situation.

He paid her rent because she had stopped working and wasn't able to keep up with her bills. And he pushed her to go to the gym to work out with him when she just wanted to stay home and die. He brought her food or took her out to eat when she wouldn't do it on her own. He was a true friend! But Joey didn't want to be her friend. He was madly in love with her and wanted to leave his family for her. And even thought she needed him, she wouldn't allow that to happen.

Chapter 9

One night, while she was home all alone, with no children to care for or a boyfriend to keep her company, she decided, instead of sitting around feeling sorry for herself, she would go out and try to meet someone to break up the redundancy of her pathetic existence.

She took a ride in her little red sports car, to a club in Sayreville in search of a distraction to break her away from the grasp that Joey was trying to capture her in.

That was when she met him, Arnold Zimmerman, the bass player of a famous New Jersey rock band.

She had pulled up to the club in her red 944 Porsche just as he was pulling up in his little red convertible Mercedes Benz. She had no idea who he was, but thought to her self, "this guy reminds me of Dudley Moore who played Arthur the drunk millionaire playboy." He was wearing a big baggy red hat and a puffy red poets shirt and he was smoking a thin brown "More" cigarette. He had a tiny goatee and she thought he was actually very cute.

She thought to her self "I have to find out who this guy is." She just knew he was someone special that she wanted to know. She never had a problem capturing anyone's attention when she wanted it, and she wanted his attention that night. He was the perfect distraction.

She had worn a real sexy, short, tight dress with no stockings and high heels. She was very tan from the tanning beds and her nails were long and red. Her hair was platinum white and she wore blue contacts so she could see love in style.

She walked right up to him, impressing him as much as he

impressed her. By the end of the evening, they were literally boyfriend and girlfriend.

She followed him back to his mansion in Rumson and fell asleep on his king sized bed, fully dressed, while he went into another room to sleep.

When she awakened a couple hours later, he showed her around his mansion. For the next six months they were together almost everyday.

She loved motorcycles and he had a few of her favorite Harleys. He took her to several bike runs in Pennsylvania and they had so much fun together. He was famous, and everywhere he went, someone recognized him and wanted his autograph. They once drove to New Hope Pennsylvania on his bike with Ali wearing only her sneakers and her bikini bathing suit.

They made such a cute couple! The stripper and the rock star!

Ali & Arnold in New Hope

Arnold with Ali's Porsche'

He impressed her so much that she wanted to impress him back. So one night while they were at a bike run with thousands of people gathered together, she entered a hot body contest. The winner received two hundred and fifty dollars. Around sixty women competed.

He had just bought her a black t-shirt with an American flag on the front and a jean skirt with black leather ties up the sides so she would blend into the biker crowd.

She was a natural on stage, so when she got her chance to stand in front of the crowd, everyone began shouting "Raise the Flag! Raise the Flag!" So, without hesitation and a desire to please her audience, she lifted her T-shirt, exposing her bodacious 34DD breasts and causing the audience to go crazy. They began screaming "USA, USA, USA!" She won the contest, made two hundred and fifty dollars and got to impress her famous rock star boyfriend. Letting him know that she was his, well deserved trophy, a prize that he should cherish. What a night!

Ali's family adored him. He wasn't a stuck up celebrity.

He was a lot of fun and had endless energy. He really enjoyed crabbing in Jessica's backyard on a pier that led to the bay and was there constantly.

One day, while Arnold and Ali were eating dinner at the Warf Inn in Deal NJ, he got on his knee in front of the entire restaurant and proposed marriage to her. He took off his gold nugget ring and put it on her finger and she said yes. But then she told him, " I really don't think that you're going to be my husband though. I didn't see you in my crystal ball".

Can you believe it? Engaged to a rock star!

Ali got to meet the entire band and their families and even flew out to L.A with Arnold for a coming out party for his friends first solo album. She stayed at his friend's house in Malibu. And she even went to the MTV awards in his bands limo with the band and wound up on national TV that night.

Jason was writing the song "Love of Arrows" while she was staying there with Arnold.

Arnold loved to drink alcohol and within a day of being at Jason's, he had drunk an entire gallon jug of Vodka that was in Jason's bar and Jason got pissed at him.

She believes to this day that a line in his song "Love of Arrows" is about her and Arnold. "A bottle of vodka in my arms, some blonde had a bad night and yeah, she's still on my couch." It may not be true, but you can't convince her of that.

After they stayed at Jason's for a few days, they drove to Dave Martins, their managers home, then to Laguna Beach.

She had a great time out in L.A. and everything was so exciting. But she missed her children and she just wanted to be a mother to them again. She really had no desires to be famous like Arnold. As a matter of fact, she thought it would be horrible to have no privacy in the world. After meeting some of the other celebrities at the MTV awards, she decided that kind of life was not for her. As much as she adored Arnold and respected his fame, she really wasn't "IN LOVE" with him and felt that she didn't belong there.

She didn't want to be some gold digging groupie who married him because of his lifestyle. It wasn't that important to her. She wanted to be with her children. They were her heart. No matter how much she smiled and put on the facade of being happy and carefree, she was hurting deep inside and no amount of celebrity, wealth or luxuries was going to stop the pain.

She realized that no matter where she went in the world, or who ever she would be with, it was only a temporary distraction that wouldn't last long enough for her to find any sense of contentment or peace.

She was still waiting for that man, she had seen so many times in her crystal ball. He was tall with long dark, curly hair and hazel brown eyes. She had imagined so many times, kissing his lips, breathing his breath and dying with him a thousand deaths, her eternal soul mate. She was searching for him, a musician with a beautiful voice who could play the piano and guitar. Arnold was not the one. He wasn't even close!

Who knows, maybe she was seeing a vision of Michael the Arch Angel. Someone who's not even in this realm, she often thought.

So AFTER A FEW DAYS in Laguna,

While she was lying on the couch with Arnold, she suddenly began to cry. He asked her what was wrong and she just snapped. She couldn't hold her repressed emotions back any longer and began to take it out on him.

"You want to know what's wrong? You're what's wrong! You're an asshole! I can't believe I have reduced myself to going out with someone like you just because you're famous. I must be out of my mind!" He responded by punching her in the face and he hit her chin. She started laughing, thinking out loud that she could whip his old tired ass. He got pissed off and called a limo to come get her.

So, at three in the morning, she was heading to the airport to take a plane back home to New Jersey. He had promised her that a car would be waiting at the Newark airport to drive her back to Brandon, but there was no one waiting.

She knew that if she called Joey, he would drop everything to get her, so she did, and he did. She was freezing when she got off the plane, so Joey, who loved to pamper her, took her to a local mall and bought her a new stylish, long, antique white, wool coat.

Poor Joey had been trying to compete with Arnold, and had gone out and bought himself a red Harley Davidson fat boy motorcycle. It was very impressive and she loved riding with him, he was so careful with her on the back and she felt so safe with him. He was only ten years older than her, but she felt like a child with her father protecting her.

Ali on Joeys Harley Davidson

It just so happened that while she was playing around with Arnold, Joey began seeing another stripper who was not so concerned about his marriage. And while he was sleeping with her, she went into his wallet, got his address and went to his house to tell his wife of seventeen years, that she was having an affair with her husband. What a selfish bitch! Ali thought. She knew the girl and had danced with her before. Her name was Star and she was a cokehead to say the least. Ali warned Joey that she was not good for him, but he had to learn for himself. She was truly a gold-digger!

WHEN ALI WAS ON THE plane heading back to New Jersey, she had a vision or premonition of Arnold being in a car accident. So, when she got back home, the next day, she decided to call his mom to tell her about it. Apparently, the woman must have believed her, because two weeks later when Arnold got back into town, he showed up at Ali's condo at 1:30 AM demanding for her to tell him everything she saw. His mother had told him about her phone call.

Arnold told her that it wasn't nice to do that to his mother, that she had gotten so upset from it, she had to take two Percocet's that night to get to sleep. Ali just laughed and said, "Why would she believe anything I say? I'm just a crazy person!"

Chapter 10

Early one morning, a year after her children had been taken from her. Ali was scheduled to work at Down The Hatch. She was home in her bathroom getting ready for work with curlers in her hair, putting makeup on her face, when she got a knock at her front door. It was around 8:30 AM.

She went down stairs and opened the door to find several plain clothed detectives standing there with badges around their necks. One of them was a woman. They asked, "Are you Alisha Durant?" She said, "I am". "You are under arrest for the "conspiracy to commit aggravated sexual assault, conspiracy to commit sexual assault, extortion, accomplice to aggravated sexual assault, accomplice to sexual assault and accomplice to endangering the welfare of a minor."

At first she thought they were joking. That this was one of those weird shows where they try to get you with some stupid joke. But they told her that it wasn't a joke. It was for real. Their guns definitely did not look like props to her.

She asked them if she could finish getting ready and make a phone call. They said it would be Ok, so she went back upstairs, took the rollers out of her hair and finished getting herself ready, while they waited downstairs in the living room.

Then right before she left with them, she called her agent Anne and told her she wasn't going to be able to make it to Down the Hatch that day.

Anne got very upset and started to yell at her for not keeping her booking as she had always done before. What could she tell her, but the truth, "I'm under arrest!" That's all she said before she hung up the phone and went off with them.

Ali doesn't remember if they handcuffed her that day, but it was the first time since it all began, that she even had a clue as to what was really going on with her children and Fenton Noor.

She had absolutely no idea that they had been putting the pieces together to create a story feasible enough to convince a jury to indict her on such insane charges.

She was now going to get a lesson taught to her about the Justice System in this country.

They say that you're innocent until proven guilty. The truth is, you're guilty when you're accused of something and if you don't have a good attorney, lots of money and an iron clad alibi, you're completely screwed!

Hell, even with an alibi your usually screwed. Just ask all the innocent people being let out of jail now since DNA testing began.

Ali sat in jail for ten days until Joey gave Jessica a thousand dollars to bail her out.

Her life was now completely over in Lexington County. They had plastered her name all over the front page of the local newspapers. "Brandon mother prostitutes seven year old to men".

"Can they do that?" she thought. Isn't there a law against News Media lying to the public? Ali had everyone she knew, wanting to know what really happened. How humiliating! The sad thing was, that everyone she thought knew her well enough, like her agent, to know that she would never do anything that disgusting, didn't believe she was innocent one bit. They believed the media. Wow! Can people really be that easily deceived? She thought. That's scary!

This world is so dangerous! People just want to believe the worst of other people. And for good reason! But didn't anyone realize that her children were so sacred to her? The only innocence she had left in this corrupt world that had already demoralized her.

If she could have, she would have kept all of her children pure and without blemish, for their entire lives.

No one knew, nor did they care. They just saw what they wanted to see, a pedophile and a stripper. Guilty by association!

She really didn't care what those deceived people thought of her anyway. She knew that there was no way on God's green earth, or in hell for that matter, that she would ever do anything to intentionally hurt ANY child on this planet, let alone her own.

She may be eccentric with weird superstitions and beliefs, but nothing that would include the victimization of innocent little children. The only evil fantasies she ever had pertained to the assassination of all the men who had ever hurt her in this life.

In her mind, anyone who believed the lies of Satan were followers of Satan himself and were as evil as the pedophile who had taken away her only daughter's innocence and traumatized her.

The negative energies surrounding Ali began to suffocate her. She needed to escape the oppression, if only for a short time, so she could breath again.

With the help of Joey, she packed up all of her belongings in the condo, put everything into storage and moved to Somerset County, which was, many miles north of where she had been living. She rented a room from a nice African American family, who had placed an ad for a tenant in the local paper. She told them her name was Sandy and they didn't bother to check her ID. So for the following year she lived as Sandy. She dyed her hair brown and went out to several local Go-Go bars in the area to get some more work.

Her stage name became "Barley Shief." She chose the name Barley from her favorite food "Mushroom Barley Soup" and Shief after her grandmother's maiden name. Would you believe she actually found a road with the same name while she was living there?

You would think that with having to juggle all her alias

names, that she would have slipped up at one point and gotten busted by someone, but she never did. She kept the names straight because she lived them. Always on stage no matter where she was.

She lived in Somerset for an entire year before going to trial and spent everyday as if it were her last days to be alive.

She rode her bike through the beautiful countryside, hung out in artsy New Brunswick and continued to visit her children every week in Waldwick, never failing to bring them Pizza or Chinese food.

It became a ritual. She was watching them grow up without her. It was two years from the time they were taken, until the trial. Tyler was six by then, and Amanda was almost ten.

The reason Ali had chosen Somerset County to runaway and hide in until her trial was because...

Chapter 11

$\sim\!\!\sim\!\!\sim\!\!\sim\!\!\sim\!\!\sim\!\!\sim\!\!\sim\!\!\sim\!\!\sim\!\!\sim\!\!\sim\!\!\sim$

While gazing into her crystal ball, she saw him again. He stood six foot-two with long dark curly hair that he wore tied back in a ponytail that fell half way down his back. He had the most beautiful, hazel eyes and she could hear his song playing in her mind, so soft and gentle. He was a singer with such a mysteriously haunting voice. But he wasn't just a singer. He was a composer who wrote the sweetest, melodious music she'd ever heard. She knew somehow that he wasn't married with any children and liked to believe that he was waiting for her to find him again. He was her soul twin. She kissed his lips and breathed his breath and died with him a thousand deaths.

In the beginning of time when God sent man to this realm, they came as one soul embryo and somehow got split apart in their journey, losing each other as they became male and female. Traveling separately through time and learning through experiences. Than, in the end they shall join as one again to become whole and androgynous as we once were before we came to Earth. At least that's what she used to believe, until she found him.

It was a cold autumn day in September of 1991. Alisha had decided to take a drive north and try to use her psychic gift to find this man who had been haunting her visions for as long as she could remember. She asked the spirits to lead her to where she could find him. In her little red 944 Porsche she drove up the New Jersey Parkway to route 287 North. She drove past the exit to New Brunswick, the college town, and felt the compelling need to get off an exit just past there. It led her down a peaceful scenic country road with lots of farmland and wooded area. There was an old rundown, dilapidated white building that looked like it had been there for a hundred years or more and left alone to ware with time.

She noticed a narrow road next to the abandoned shack and turned to follow it. On her right was a swamp that was so close to the road one wrong move with the steering wheel would have caused the car to fall into it. She wondered how anyone ever drove down this road in the rain, at night, or when they were tired without winding up in that marsh.

As she followed the lane, she felt an overwhelming feeling that she was close. Her heart began beating faster with the anticipation of finding him. The trees around her began to change and hover over the quiet empty street. They looked as though they had all grown towards the road as if some strange energy was pulling them all in that direction. The trees were bare of leaves, dark and twisted like they had been in some peculiar war with the elements that surrounded them. If it had been night she thought to herself, she would have been very scared, because it was actually spooky in some obscured way!

She past a couple ranch houses on the left and noticed fenced in property with a no trespassing sign on her right. Apparently there was some sort of private nature reserve there. Then she thought to herself "Where to hell am I? I must be out of my mind to be thinking I'm actually going to find anyone way out here in the middle of nowhere."

Then she came to an old red brick house with tree's almost hiding it from view and noticed another red brick house sitting in the back behind it. The houses were surrounded by a cyclone fence, which had a gate to close out unwanted visitors. She turned into the driveway as she noticed the gate was opened and stopped to try to get another feeling of what to do or where to go next.

Then it happened…

A BLACK JEEP WRANGLER WITH the top down appeared out of nowhere accelerating down the stone driveway then suddenly stopped at her car. She jumped out of her Porsche and went right over to greet him without any reserve. Ali immediately noticed that he wore the hair, but couldn't see his face too clearly because he had sunglasses on.

Her first words to him were "Can you take off your glasses?" He did so without question and the next thing she said to this stranger whom she had never seen before in this lifetime was, "Do you know that I've been searching for you for the past one hundred and twenty years?"

He laughed loudly then asked her "What psychiatric hospital did you just escape from?" She realized how insane she must have sounded to him and decided to use her womanly charm to warm him up to her, instead of just blowing his mind and winding up with a restraining order put on her.

She saw that he had his dog in the jeep sitting next to him and asked him where he was headed. He said "to the park" and asked her if she would like to follow him there. He was curious as to who this woman was, who suddenly appeared out of nowhere, to claim that she had been searching for him for over a century. He also couldn't help but to notice that she was very attractive, and her car was not one that a desperate crazy person might be driving. At least he didn't think so.

She followed behind his jeep as he led her to a park not far from his home. He let his dog run around for a while and hit her with a ton of questions. Who are you? Where did you come from? How did you find me? What do you want? He seemed to be very suspicious and yet intrigued at the same time.

She wanted to tell him everything that she knew, but didn't want to overwhelm him. He told her his name was Francis, but everyone called him Franc. They eventually went back to his house. She wasn't allowed in the front house because that was where his parents lived and he didn't want to disturb them. He invited her into the back house where he told her he was staying.

She was amazed at what she saw as she entered into his

den. There was a nicely framed pencil drawing of Marilyn Monroe on the wall. Only it didn't look that much like Marilyn, it looked more like her. Then she glanced over at him with questioning eyes and he answered, "That's my true love!" Then he took Ali by the hand like an excited little boy showing off his toys, and led her into his recording studio that he had set up in the front room. He sat her down on one of the swivel chairs and turned on his computer that attached to his equipment. A song began to play. "Time find a way for me, to find my way to her, oh I need time." Then he played "Two broken hearts" and several other songs that he had written and performed. She couldn't believe how talented he was.

"How is it that I've never heard of you?" she asked him. He told her that he used to be in several bands that made albums, but it was fifteen years before. He also told her he was only thirty-four. Ali didn't think he was any younger and liked the idea of being with an older man. It wouldn't have mattered if he were older.

She really didn't like to pry into other people's personal lives, but she was curious if he were telling the truth about his age. So she closed her eyes and focused on his driver's license, then she saw the number fifty-one in her mind. She told him this and he admitted to her that he had been born in 1951, which made him forty-one at that time. Ali admitted to him that she was psychic and reminded him that he didn't have to lie to her about his age.

She couldn't help but to notice that the only room in his house that was clean was the one with his recording studio set up in it. The rest of the house looked like a tornado had hit it. The bathrooms looked like they hadn't been cleaned in five years, and he even confessed that to her.

She thought to her self, "Wow, this guy is really eccentric! He must be a musical genius who just focuses on his music and pays no attention to anything else around him."

Ali had tried to envision a date when they would be married and she thought she saw the year 1994. That date was only a couple years away. Then she thought to herself that if they were going to be man and wife in the near future, they could just skip the intros and get right down to the commitments. But it didn't work that way. You can't force a vision to happen when YOU want it too. It will happen when it's meant to happen, if it happens at all in the present life.

She left his house without meeting his parents that night, not even a kiss goodbye, and drove back home. He had given her a CD of his music to listen to while she drove. She thought about a poem she had once written envisioning when she finally found her true love. She felt that something tragic would happen and she would lose him again. These words were how it would be when her search for this lost soul mate was over.

As I'm driving down the highway
Teardrops falling from my eyes
I think about the love I lost
And that dream of Mr. Right
I listen to the tape I have
It's the only sound I know
Of the music that he gave me once
To listen to as go
In my little red Porsche as I'm cruising really fast
I'm thinking about the memories of all the times that have past
Fading dreams and yesterday
The time has come to go
And put an end to this fantasy of being with a ghost
Sorrow as I come to an end
Just thought that you should know
There are palm trees in my paradise
And that's where I think I'll go
Good-bye! I love you!
Gray skies and crying eyes
The dream is gone!

She wondered if she was now living her premonition and couldn't believe he was real. She had seen him countless times in her visions and thought that he might not even be of this realm. Why did it, take until now to find him, she wondered.

What did it all mean? Was he going to be the one to rescue her or was this just another pathetic chapter in her life that had to play itself out for some cosmic reason? All she knew was that she didn't want to leave him. EVER! She had finally found him and wanted to become one with him again, but she knew that she had to go back to reality to survive.

When she got back home, she called him and conversed with him for a while. It was around midnight when they finally hung up. She was so over tired and restless. It had been such a long day and a wild adventure. "So now what?" She thought to herself as she closed her eyes and slowly drifted off to sleep.

Chapter 12

A week had gone by. Ali had been working in the strip clubs as usual. She had been invited to the Count Basie Theater in Red Bank for a benefit play that was being put on for one of her friends. She had been looking forward to this event for some time, but was now really excited to think that Franc might be there as well. Seems he also knew the guy they were throwing the benefit for. When she got to the theater, to her surprise, Adam Sr. was there with his newly wed wife. Holy crap! Adam had finally taken the plunge after all those years. And he didn't even marry Sasha who he had lived with for thirteen of those years. His wife's name was Mary and she seemed like a very sweet girl. Ali was really happy for them both.

Her friend Tanya, who was with the theater group, asked Ali if she wouldn't mind helping them out with a skit. Ali thought it would be fun to be acting on stage at the famous Count Basie. She got her lines to read and studied them briefly, then, went with the rest of the actors behind the stage to prepare for her performance. This was the first and only time that Ali ever acted on stage. And guess whom she played? Marilyn!

Franc was out in the audience watching her in amusement as she sat at a table on stage with other performers to act out a skit. After it was over, she caught up with him out in the lobby. Someone they knew wanted to take a photograph of the two of them together and Ali thought it would be great to capture their first kiss on film and she somehow managed to get it.

As he bent down to kiss her lips, the photo was taken. He took her breath away and she melted right on camera. It was the most passionate first kiss that would be remembered forever.

Ali had asked Franc prior if he would escort her to the event, but apparently he had another date for that night with someone else. The jealousy stung her, but what could she do? She had just found him again and couldn't really expect him to change his life now that she was in it. His date was with someone he was hoping could help him get a record deal with some major recording company. Turns out, Franc was not that impressed with his date and wound up hanging out with Ali after all for the remainder of the evening.

They sat in his jeep in the parking lot for a little while and she lie in his arms kissing his lips again. This began a chapter in her life that she had hoped would never end. If it were up to her, she would have stayed in his arms that night forever. She just wanted to climb inside of him and become one with him again because the pain of their separation was too unbearable. But the night was almost over and they both had to get back to their homes. So they eventually parted ways.

The next night they spoke for nearly two hours on the phone. He had given her hope that they would soon be together again. A few hours later, around 3:30 AM, Ali was awakened by a peculiar phone call. "Hello?" she answered "Hi! Is this Ali?" the voice replied. "Yes it is." "Hi this is Francs mother." Hi! Ali was surprised to be hearing from his mother so late at night, and thought it was very weird that this woman, who didn't even know her, would choose such a late hour to call and introduce her self.

But then, she thought that it must be normal for them to stay up so late. Ali envisioned Franc's parents as partiers, since they shared the same life with him and he seemed like he enjoyed the Night Life a lot. She thought that it was very nice to have received a phone call from his mother introducing herself no matter what the hour was.

But then panic set in when the next words Ali heard from the phone were, "I'm sorry to be calling you so late, but Franc had an accident tonight and is in the hospital being operated on." "WHAT? Oh my God! I just talked to him a few hours ago. He had an accident? OH MY GOD! " All Ali kept thinking was how she spent her entire life searching for this man and when she finally found him, something tragic would happen that would take him away from her again. "Is he Ok?" Ali asked. "He broke his arm very badly and they had to put a metal plate in to hold it together. Franc asked me to call you and tell you that he's going to be in the hospital for a few days." Ali asked her what hospital he was in and at 3:45 AM she was out of bed, showering and getting ready to head to New Brunswick to be with her wounded soul mate.

As she drove to the hospital, she thought to herself, "It's only a broken arm, he'll survive. He's going to need someone to nurture him though until he's better." Ali loved to nurture her men. This was going to be a nice experience, she thought.

She arrived at the hospital around 6 AM and entered through the emergency room. There was only one couple sitting on the chairs in the waiting area. Ali assumed that it must be his parents, so she apprehensively approached them and asked, "Are you Franc's parents?" His mother answered her very kindly with a yes.

Ali was completely blown away by their appearance. "Wow, and I thought I was eccentric! These are my kind of people. Maybe they will even like me." She thought. She really hadn't actually tried to envision what his parents might look like, but this peculiar couple, was not at all what she could have ever imagined in her wildest fantasies.

His mother was somewhat short and fairly overweight and she was wearing these tight, white spandex pants that showed off the excessive amounts of bulky cellulite under her clothes. She had a large pear shaped body and wore high-heeled shoe boots that at first glance reminded Ali of an elephant on roller skates. She had a short, tight, purple tank top on that practically exposed her entire flabby upper torso and her hair was extremely long, red and curly. It stuck out on all ends like she had put her finger into a light socket. Her makeup was bright blue eye shadow, thick black eye liner, deep, red rough and bright red lipstick. Ali had wondered if this woman was putting her makeup on in the dark. "Did she even know how she looked? It was worse than Bozo the clown." She thought. WOE! Ali would never disrespect anyone by mentioning her perceptions of them to anyone else, so she just accepted it and then put it out of her mind.

Franc's father was completely the opposite of his mother, who, for an older lady appeared to be trying very hard to look young and sexy. He was also very short and fifteen years older than his wife. He looked like an old farmer wearing big, baggy pants with suspenders, work boots and a red flannel shirt. He also wore glasses that were perfect for someone of his age and gender. His folks seemed nice enough, but Ali couldn't help wondering how this very small, peculiar couple could spawn such a tall, handsome son. It was amazing to see such a genetic contrast between them.

Together they all went up to Franc's room after he had finished in recovery. He had an I.V. in his right hand with a morphine drip to stop the pain and he was wearing a purple cast on his left arm that was elevated in some sort of hanging splint. His hair was out of its usual ponytail and he was looking as regal as ever in his light-blue hospital gown. He was lying down with his eyes closed and when he opened them was surprised to find everyone hovering around his bed, especially Ali. He was trying hard not to look embarrassed of his situation, and it did him no good to be proud while wasted on such a powerful narcotic, so he just gave in letting his defenses down to go with the flow.

He formally introduced everyone to each other and then blatantly mentioned that he had to pee. Ali helped him to slowly and carefully get out of his bed and she put his I.V. on a pole with wheels, so he could drag it to the bathroom beside him. He went inside the fairly large room with his arm in a sling to pee. But after a few unsuccessful minutes he began yelling that he couldn't go. He wanted Ali to help him. So, she went into the bathroom and stood next to him to hold his penis over the toilet bowl. She held it there for a long while trying to help him express himself. His entire back was exposed and Ali couldn't help but to notice what a cute ass he had under his long hospital robe. She also couldn't believe that she had spent one hundred and twenty years searching for this man who was now standing next to her in a hospital bathroom crying that he couldn't pee while he had her holding his penis over a toilet. What a way to get to know someone, huh?

She was captivated by his vulnerability and his strong uninhibited desire for her to play nursemaid to his immediate needs. A perfect match made in Heaven!

Ali was very tired after her visit from lack of sleep and was hoping that Franc's parents would invite her to their house to get some rest before she had to make that long trip back to Brandon, back to her lonely life without her children. But they never offered and she didn't want to intrude, so as tired as she was, she made the trip home and went to sleep.

In the morning she had a gig at Down the Hatch and while she was getting herself ready for work, the doorbell rang. It was the police, there to arrest her for the sexual assault of her daughter Amanda. Ali spent the next two weeks in the county jail and all she could think about was Franc and how she had finally found him.

He had left the hospital a couple days after her arrest and accepted all of her collect calls to him at his home. Back then, there was no time limit on calls from jail so Ali spent endless hours on the phone getting to know him and falling deeper in love with him than she had ever imagined happening. Franc's phone bill that month was nearly a thousand dollars thanks to Ali.

When Joey gave Jessica the money to bail Ali out of jail, all she could think about was getting closer to Franc. She was trying not to dwell on the reality of what was really happening around her and she fell deeper into her mental escape with the fantasy of this man from 1872.

Ali used the excuse that her life was over in Lexington County, because of the scandalous newspaper articles they had written about her. Then she talked Joey into helping her put most of her stuff into storage and move her to Somerset County. Her apartment was only six miles from Franc and she spent much of the following year, the year before her trial, with him in his recording studio.

Chapter 13

She didn't know how much time she had left to be with him and desperately wanted to believe that she would be found innocent so her vision would come true of her marriage to him in 1994. She couldn't help but to feel like she was under a spell. Perhaps one of her own doing, but every time she was with him, she had that déjà vu feeling that she was back in the 1800's. A moment in time when there was romance, honor and chivalry. Was she really just trying to escape reality or could it all have been possible?

She only wanted to sit in a white Winsor rocking chair and do needlepoint as she watched her fantasy fiancé create the most beautiful music in his studio. So she set out to fulfill her destiny by cleaning his house, scrubbing down the bathrooms and doing everything she could for him. She even bought an unfinished Winsor rocker that she hand painted white and put in his den. She bought him a new mattress and box spring for his bed with matching designer sheets and comforter, scrubbed his floors, did his dishes and played house with him as much as she could. She even bought two ten-speed mountain bikes so they could ride through the scenic county side together. Ali lived every moment with him as if it were going to be their last together in this life.

But something was off with him and she just couldn't figure it out. Sometimes she would question whether or not he was really the one she had been searching for. He seemed to have several different personalities and at times was really nasty. He was overly paranoid about someone coming to his house to hurt him, expose his secrets or just invade his personal space. He had surveillance cameras and sensor lighting all around the perimeter of his house for warning.

Ali watched as his friends would drive all the way to his house from afar to visit him and he wouldn't even answer his door. They knew he was home because his jeep would be parked outside, and they would knock for a long while with no response. Eventually they would leave. He would call the front house practically every fifteen minutes to check up on his parents and did that even in the middle of the night when they were both most likely sleeping. Something was just not right. Had she made a mistake? Was this really the guy from 1872 who was going to marry her in 1994? There was something about him that really bothered her.

When they made love, and Ali closed her eyes, she would always see that white piano and the plantation house with the four-post bed in her mind. She saw other images of him as well and began to piece them all together one image at a time, until one night, while they lie in his bed, he spoke to her in a voice that she clearly recognized.

"I know who you are!" she said to him, as she sat up, distancing herself from him. "

"You're Luther! Martin Luther!" the so-called great reformer. And the reason you're so damn paranoid in this life is because you're afraid someone is going to recognize you. And you're right, because I do. But don't worry, I won't tell anyone. No one would believe me anyway. You contributed to the death of thousands of Jews. It was your words that Hitler quoted as he massacred all those people! You should be ashamed of yourself!" she said to him.

But he wasn't Luther, he was Franc the composer. She suddenly remembered that Luther loved to write music also and wrote one of the most powerful hymns ever known to man, (The Mighty Fortress). Luther was a miserable person who would lock himself away for days writing sermons, just like Franc would lock himself away to write his music. He married a Nun and had a bunch of children. It's no wonder he didn't want any in this life. "Oh my God, I'm going crazy!" she cried as she got out his bed and tried to leave.

He grabbed her and held her down, telling her that she couldn't leave him. "LET ME GO!" she screamed as she threw her clothes on and ran towards the front door. He slammed her against the wall and tried to hold her there. She broke loose and ran to the kitchen sink and grabbed two kitchen knives that were just sitting in there. She held them out to him, one in each hand and warned him not to come near her. He didn't listen and attempted to grab her. She stuck one of them into his leg and he backed away giving her enough time to get out of his house. She ran to her car and jumped inside, still holding the knives in her hands. She turned the engine on and threw it in gear as quickly as she could and bolted down his driveway. Her hands were shaking out of control and she was completely out of breath from fear. She drove back to her apartment and locked herself inside.

A few minutes later Franc was banging at her door, begging her to let him in. She screamed for him to go away, but he wouldn't leave. "Please let me come inside. I won't hurt you, I promise." He sounded so sweet and desperate. "Remember 1872!" he said to her through the locked door. Against her better instincts, she unlocked the door to let him come inside. As soon as he got in, his voice changed again. "You little Bitch! I'm going to make you pay for this! Look what you did to me!" He grabbed her by her hair and swung her onto the bed. It just so happened, that she kept a double-edged dagger under her pillow for moments like this when she would need it. She grabbed the dagger and held it in his face threatening to stab him again if he didn't go away. So he left. And she cried herself to sleep not knowing who or where to turn to next.

Ali didn't see him again for a few days after that until things cooled down and they both began to miss each other. Then she got a page "1872", it was him and he loved her! He had promised her once a long time ago that he would never leave her. She loved him with all her heart. He was her soul twin. They would be married in 1994. She had to go back.

Ali painted him a picture on canvas with her acrylic paints. It was of a watch suspended in clouds. She named it "Time." Just like the song he had written. She brought it to his house and hung it over his bed and was back in her rocking chair working on her tapestry of him, her man from 1872. It wasn't long before she was slashing the painting with a knife and running out of his house again as he changed personalities that would abuse her in some obscured way and drain her psychic energies.

They would ride their bikes in the country and fight constantly like two children with sibling rivalry. He was just as crazy as she was because he believed her as much as she believed what she believed. He wanted to be famous and he wanted her to be famous, but she wasn't into the fame thing. She wanted Love! His love! She had already been famous in her last life and it didn't make her happy then, why would it make anyone happy, she thought. It's just too bad that he had to miss it, but she wasn't going to try to do it again. All he kept saying to her over and over again was "get me a record deal." She was a stripper not a businessman. She couldn't MAKE someone famous if it wasn't there destiny to become famous.

THE ONE MOMENT IN TIME where she was completely in awe of his love for her was when she was dancing on stage at a strip club somewhere in Bound brook. She had asked the DJ to play her CD of Franc's music. It went perfect with her style of dance and she was completely in flow with his song when she looked down to find him sitting at the bar watching her gracefully and seductively moving to the sound of his voice. She felt like she was in a dream, and never wanted to wake up. The stage and in his presents were the only two places she could go where she could forget everything horrible that was happening in her life. She could forget reality and live in her fantasy. That was her safe haven and now he was a part of it.

She loved him more than anyone else in this world other than her children. But was it really Love or just obsession with someone she had created in her imagination? It was as if she had designed some character from a story and searched out a man to play his part. He was the perfect lead in her novel of love and romance. But there was a dark side to that love, some hidden agenda that she couldn't quite figure out. He was hiding something from her.

She wanted to stay in his world and never leave, but it was a world so far from her own. She wished that her children were with her in that other world, but she couldn't be with them and she had to accept it.

Only once did she take him for a ride to meet her family. They had driven far and when they got close to her sister's house, he cried, "Stop the car!" Then he jumped out and refused to go any farther with her. "What is wrong with you?" she demanded. "I thought you wanted to meet my family? My parents are there today so you can meet them both." For some reason, he thought that someone was going to be there to hurt him. He thought that maybe Joey was her boyfriend and that he was going to be there to beat him up. Ali finally convinced him to get back in the car after reassuring him over and over again that there was no danger. Her parent's only met Franc once and he never went with her again into her world.

She went back to the hypnotist to find out what had happened back in 1872 and how her "true love" had died. She thought that Franc's fears were somehow connected to that lifetime and she was right.

Chapter 14

The year was 1872...
Elizabeth's father could no longer take care of her. He was a blacksmith who made very little money and had to work long hours to barely survive. Her mother had died from the Yellow Fever and left them alone. It was in the best interest of the child that she went to live with her aunt who could provide a decent home for her until she was of age. It wasn't proper that a girl be left alone at home most of the time. She needed a mother to teach her to become a woman.

Elizabeth's aunt was a church going woman who belonged to the social community. She brought Elizabeth to her friend Anne's house one day for tea and that's when she caught the eye of Rylan, Anne's grandson. Rylan was betrothed to Rebecca, they say from birth. Apparently the two families were very wealthy and wanted to combine their fortunes with the bonding of their children. Rylan had grown up with Rebecca and thought of her more like a sister. When he and Elizabeth met, they immediately took to each other.

He loved to play the piano and enjoyed entertaining Elizabeth who had never heard anyone play a musical instrument before. She was fascinated with him and appreciated his talent. Rebecca thought that he was foolish for wasting his time with such folly and thought that he should be spending more time with her father learning their family business.

It was customary that Rylan join the military when he became of age. When his time came, he spent three years away. During which time he wrote to Elizabeth constantly. They fell in love through their writing. He also wrote to Rebecca, but again, he thought of her more like the sister he never had.

As soon as he got out of the military, he was suppose to marry Rebecca. Her family had thrown a huge ball at their mansion and that was when he was suppose to officially ask Rebecca for her hand in marriage. It was their official engagement party.

Elizabeth was home that night, sitting in the dark crying from a broken heart. She was so in love with Rylan and thought that he loved her too, but there was no way that he was going to defy his family and ruin the plans that everyone had worked so hard to establish. She was almost sure that she didn't mean that much to him.

But then, she heard the sound of horses outside her window pulling a coach. She went to the door to see who might be visiting her at such a late hour. And to her surprise it was her beloved Rylan. As he stepped out of the coach she could see that he was wearing his stately uniform looking proud and regal. Her insides filled with excitement to see him again for the first time since he left years before. "What are you doing here?" she asked with surprise. He quietly walked over to her putting his arms so tightly around her that you would think he were holding on for dear life and didn't say a word. He just looked down into her eyes feeling lifetimes of love for her and kissed all of her sorrows away.

After he finished absorbing years of desire from her, he answered her question. "I went to the ball tonight and when the time came to get on bended knee to ask for Rebecca's hand in marriage, all I could see was your face, drenched in tears. I don't love her the way that I love you. I have spent countless nights dreaming of kissing your lips and breathing your breath and holding you in my arms as MY wife. " As he said those words to her, he dropped down on one knee, with her hands in his hands he looked up at her and spoke these gentle words " I am so sorry Elizabeth for making you question my love for you. Never again will I ever put anyone or anything before our love. It would do me a great honor if you would accept my hand

and become my wife. That is if you still love me as much as I love you. Please Elizabeth…Will you marry me?"

She was absolutely convinced that she had fallen asleep and was dreaming all of this. There was no way that Rylan, who stood to inherit a small fortune when he married Rebecca, would give it all up for some poor blacksmiths lonely daughter. Was it even possible that this well educated, talented, handsome man could actually love someone so beneath him?

It wasn't a dream! He was there and he was real and he just asked her to marry him. Her reply was " I hope if this is a dream that I never wake up from it. It would be my dream come true to be married to you Rylan. Of course I WILL! I do love you with all my heart.

Then he slipped the ring that was meant for Rebecca onto HER hand. He told her that when he got that ring, he tried to imagine what it would look like on her hand and not Rebecca's. He said that Rebecca wouldn't even appreciate a ring like that. Elizabeth thought it was the most beautiful ring she had ever seen and it most likely was.

A couple days later, while Rylan was in town, a few guys jumped him and beat him senselessly. They left him lying in the street all busted up. He was carried to the Doctors office and put on his examination table for observation. Elizabeth's Aunt just happened to be near by and heard what had happened. Turns out, Rebecca's family was not that happy with the news of his engagement to someone other than their Rebecca. And it was her brother and a few cousins that caught him by surprise. It was five against one. That wasn't very fair.

As soon as Rylan healed from his wounds, they were married in a small white chapel on the outskirts of town. It was a quaint wedding with only a few family members who attended. As they were leaving the church to enter the wedding coach, he stood in front of her and looked her in the eyes then said, "I promise you that I will always love you and I will never leave you!"

That night she conceived his son.

Six months later when all was quiet, Rylan got some crazy

idea in his head to get even with Rebecca's family for beating him up. He decided to burn down their red barn. Elizabeth was now six months pregnant and wanted to go with him. He was only going to make a statement. The barn was empty inside and there was only some hay and a pitchfork. He actually thought of it as a practical joke and they laughed about it. Rylan had grown up with Rebecca's family and never really thought that they would actually kill him. He said that they really weren't killer's as mad as they might get at him. So, while Elizabeth went barefoot, they trotted through a path in the woods that led to the barn. Rylan carried the kerosene can. After they lit the barn on fire, they both began to run back down the path, but Elizabeth couldn't run fast enough and before they knew it, the same guys who had beat him up the first time, came out from behind the trees and grabbed him again. One guy held Elizabeth while two other's held Rylan and two more began punching him in the face and stomach. They just kept beating on him and wouldn't stop. Elizabeth was crying for them to stop, yelling that they were going to kill him. Then, the two guys who held him let go of him at the same time and he fell to the ground, hitting his head on a rock that killed him instantly. Elizabeth ran to his side, holding him in her arms yelling for him to wake up. But he was gone. He had left her six months pregnant.

Chapter 15

After Alisha left the hypnotist, she drove to Franc's house and noticed their two bikes out on the lawn. She knew that he had been riding that day with someone and felt that it was a woman. Ali demanded that he tell her who he was with and then, out of anger, she ran the bikes over with her car. She went inside his house to get her belongings because she knew he had cheated on her and she was leaving him for the last time. The phone just happened to ring at that very moment and Ali picked up the receiver. "Hello?" she said. "Oh! Hello?" the voice replied. "Who is this?" Ali asked. "Holly." Ali knew that this was the person Franc had been with and asked Holly to meet with her. Ali told her that she just wanted to talk with her about Franc. Holly agreed to meet her at the Woodbridge Commons Mall in some café there. So before Franc came into the house to know what had transpired, Ali took off out the door to her car. She was determined to find out the truth.

When she got to the Café, she noticed a petite blonde with blue eyes wearing a peculiar hat sitting at the bar. This woman spoke with some overly soft voice that made Ali think she was just some mindless airhead. Then, she began giving this woman the third degree. Ali acted as if everything this woman told her meant nothing and that she really didn't care, but deep down inside she felt completely betrayed and deceived by Franc. Unfortunately, the more that Holly spoke, the more Ali realized that Holly was actually Rebecca, the bitch that was suppose to marry Franc when he was Rylan.

What totally convinced her that Holly was Rebecca was

when Holly told her that she had a brother who died when he committed suicide by shooting himself to death in a red barn. When you take a life, you have to give one. He must have been the one who actually killed Rylan in 1872, so he came back to give his own life to cleanse his karma. "Son of a bitch!"

Holly had been dating Franc for six years and they had only been broken up for a few months when he met Ali. But as soon as Holly found out about Ali, she wanted Franc back. And according to her, she had been seeing Franc the entire year that Ali had been with him. She had threatened suicide if he didn't see her and apparently, he felt sorry for her so he continued seeing her behind Ali's back.

Ali loved Franc, but she knew that she only had a few more weeks left before she had to go to trial. She knew that she was going to lose her case because she had no defense. A part of her wanted to go to jail just so she could try to break the spell that she was under. She thought that with time she could forget him and move on. She knew that this was how it was all going to end. It had to end! She couldn't live like this any longer, all the lies, all the hidden agendas and deception, all the past life karma that had somehow caught up with her at that very moment in time.

She followed Holly back to her apartment and as soon as they got inside, Franc showed up and began kicking Holly really hard and tearing down her curtains. He was physically abusing this little woman and Ali came to her defense. "Don't you dare touch her!" she yelled. "Leave her alone! I know everything and you have been unfaithful to me the entire time." Ali was so hurt and before she left, she told the both of them, "I am Elizabeth and Rylan will always love me no matter where I go. You can't compete with a ghost! When the two of you are riding your bikes together, I'll be there with you and you won't be able to enjoy yourselves knowing that it's me who should be with him and no one else. When your having sex in the bed that I got him, it's my face that you'll see when you close your eyes. He'll be making love to my vision, not anyone else's! I will haunt the both of you until the end of time!" Ali turned and walked out the door leaving the both of them standing there in dismay.

I've searched for you forever
I know that you're the one
We have loved each other a long time
In lifetimes that have past on
We've searched an entire existence
To find each other's love.
But like a curse we had to lose it,
To spend the rest of our lives lost because
It's gone.
In sorrow I'll wait forever
Together we belong.
If it means trying again next time
I know that I can wait that long
In this lifetime, we might not do it.
But the next will come along.
And when it does, I'll be there,
to finish our number one song.

Written by Ali

Francis the reincarnated composer

Sometimes we wish that life was like writing a book that we can finish with a happily ever after. Or begin the next chapter somewhere else, some other place that will bring us comfort and peace, sometimes we're just happy that the story ends. But that's not really how life is. It goes on even when we think that we're at the brink of insanity and we can't take one more breath of this painful, miserable, stupid existence that we are trapped in. We think that we're all alone in our suffering and that no one can help us.

It's at that moment that we need to look to the heavens and pray for God to give us the strength to go on. He WILL not try us beyond what we can stand! If we are suffering so bad that we can't even breathe, he must know something that we do not. He knows just how much we can take. Just keep going!!! Breathe!!! Take one breath at a time! Sometimes that's all we can do. Just breath because life does goes on, even when there seems to be no more reasons to live. Don't give up! We will get through the cosmic storm!

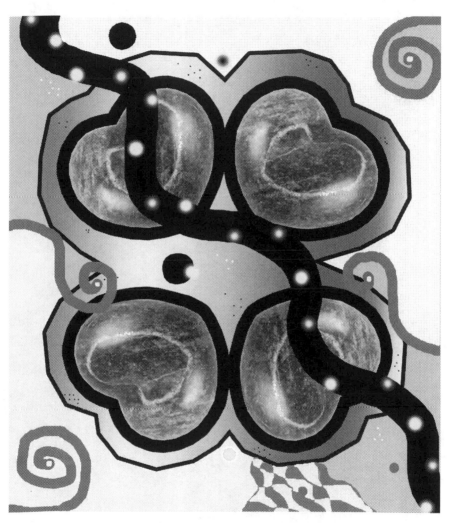

Stone Hearts

Chapter 16

Holly called Ali that very night and told her she was sorry if she had hurt her. Ali said it wasn't her fault. She had stolen Franc from her in her past life and now, she had to watch the two of them be together while she was locked behind bars. It was her destiny. But Ali didn't know how much time she would get in jail because deep in her heart she still had hope that she would be marrying him in 1994 which was only a year or so away. Ali asked her if she would be her friend and let her know how Franc was doing while she was away. Holly promised that she would do that for her.

Franc went to see Ali a few days before she went to trial and asked her if she would stay with him at a local motel. She loved him so much that she couldn't deny herself the one last moment of pleasure in this life of make love with him. No matter what had happened between them. They spent their last night together in a neutral place.

There were no more secrets to hide. No more battles to win. She had found him again and had to let him go. It was her destiny to find her true love only to lose him to the realities of her failures and he couldn't rescue her. No one could.

They held onto each other passionately kissing and breathing each other's breath. She desperately wanted to climb inside of him to become one with him again so she could be free, but it just wasn't possible. He tasted so good to her and she felt him inside of her for the last time. Tears streamed down her face, as she closed her eyes and held onto the memories of their brief moment together in this life. He had brought her to climax time and time again with his perfect, thrusting, rock hard erections, but had held out on pleasuring her in any other way.

This last night as he lie on top of her, softly kissing her warm, wet lips, he slowly and gently kissed his way down her soft, smooth body until he was kissing her thighs. Then he spread her legs farther apart and put his warm, wet mouth upon her throbbing, longing, beautiful flower. Tasting her nectar and feeling it with his mouth. He lovingly caressed her canal with his tongue, licking every erogenous zone in her area, while his hands fondled her breasts and his fingers tweaked her nipples. The endless pleasure shot through her body like an electrical shock. She let herself go and didn't hold back, as her fingers ran threw his long dark curls, she grabbed his head and let out an explosion of feelings. Her body quivered in ecstasy as her love juices got sucked down his throat.

Then he kissed his way back up her body until he reached her lips again. She grabbed his head and pushed her tongue deep into his opened mouth while tasting her self on his breath. She reached down and took his wet cock into her hand and put it to her opening as he thrust her over and over again. She called out for him to go deeper, harder, faster without stopping! "Fuck Me!" she cried "Fuck me hard!" Grabbing his ass with her hands she pulled him deeper into her as she pushed upward, until he couldn't hold back any longer. He let it all out in one passionate moan as he came inside of her while wearing a condom.

She couldn't believe how he had held back that entire year from really pleasuring her the way she liked until their last time together. Ali was really disappointed in him for that. What an asshole she thought. They could have had some really pleasurable moments, but for the most part, it was usually kissing for a few minutes until his penis got hard and then he would reach into the drawer in the nightstand next to his bed, where he always kept a stash of condoms. At least she never had to worry about getting a venereal disease from him.

Chapter 17

During the trial, Fenton's daughter testified against Ali. Painting her out to be a heartless prostitute that would bring men back to her condo for paid sex. But how did she know that, when Ali had never even spoken a word to her except on the phone, one time while she was at the prosecutor's office? His daughter didn't even know who Ali was by sight until the trial. Her testimony was purely hearsay coming from most likely her father's stories.

Fenton was just a jealous, scorned pedophile who, only fantasized about what Ali did. He had no real proof, because there was none. No men to come forward to say that they had slept with her for money. There were no photographs, no taped conversations or nothing at all that could prove what he was saying was true, because it wasn't true. She never told him those things either, nor could he prove it in any way if she did. His testimony was merely hearsay as well. But for some reason he had more credibility than Ali in the courtroom.

There was even an incident at the Body Language strip club several months after her children had been taken from her. She really didn't think much of it at the time, but was sure it had some significance to her case.

She was dancing as usual on stage, when a customer sitting behind the bar called her over to show her six hundred dollars that he had placed in front of himself. He told her to take it if she would be with him that night.

He was not a very attractive man and quite overweight to say the least. Ali immediately got a bad feeling from it, turned around and jumped back up on stage. She danced around for a few more minutes trying to analyze the situation in her head. No one had ever done that to her before.

It suddenly occurred to her what it was about. So she approached him again, this time picking up the money and counting it. There was exactly six hundred dollars in her hands.

She looked at the fat, bald, homely man wearing glasses, with complete contempt for insulting her intelligence, and said to him "I want you to go back down town and tell your friends at the prosecutors office, that if they want to set me up for prostitution, they better send someone a hell of a lot better looking than you!"

She thought too much of herself to allow her body to be touched by someone unworthy of her affections. She was more of an exhibitionist. She didn't mind them looking if they paid, just don't touch her or you might get a bottle thrown in your face!

Trust me, she was not about being touched by anyone, much less a paying customer! She had already lost respect for the men in this world who she knew were married and hanging out in the strip clubs trying to get laid by the strippers.

She would sometimes secretly fantasize about dressing up in her camouflage costume with an Uzi strapped to her shoulder, a string of bullets wrapped around her like in the movies. With no one thinking that it was real, just a prop she had designed for her show.

Then, on a Saturday night when the bar was so crowded that there wasn't even standing room, she would get up on the stage to perform, and take her Uzi off her shoulder, load a strand of bullets and just start blasting everyone sitting around the bar.

All the cheating men who left their wives at home to take care of their spoiled, bratty children. While the wives got abused and neglected by them, they're out sleazing in the bars trying to pick up whoever would be willing to stoop to their level.

It really was a good thing that Ali went to jail when she did, she had been pushed to her limits, especially with a man touching her sweet innocent little girl. She would have done something sooner or later to get even. If she couldn't get even with Fenton himself, she most likely would have taken it out on some other sick fuck!

Ali knew this, deep inside, and that's one of the reasons she didn't fight to defend her self. Karma would take care of it, she always thought. It always does! Sooner or later what goes around comes around.

AT THE TRIAL, PEGGY THE other babysitter testified and painted a picture of a woman who had no lights in the kid's bedroom for them to see and no food in the house for them to eat. Basically saying that Ali was a selfish, uncaring woman who neglected her children's basic needs.

The reason the babysitter thought there were no lights, is because the obese, lazy, homely bitch, tried only the light switch next to the bedroom door.

The light never turned on from the switch! You had to actually enter the room and turn on the light from the lamp, the beautiful, two hundred dollar, lamp that the children had, on their expensive dresser. In a room that was mostly windows and skylights, that lit up the room brightly just from the moonlight. People would comment on Ali's condo: that it was well decorated and the children didn't want for anything.

But the worst lie that that vindictive bitch told the jury, was that when she called Ali to tell her that her poor daughter had been molested by Fenton, Ali had said to her, "Amanda probably deliberately took off her panties and sat on his face." What a fucking liar! That is truly bearing false witness against your neighbor, literally! Exodus 20:16 Ali is still waiting to hear what kind of Karmic retribution she had to pay. There is a God in heaven watching over us!

The reason that the babysitter thought there was no food in the house for them to eat, most likely, was because Ali never kept junk food around. She believed in eating only healthy foods. So when Peggy babysat for them, *only one night*, at her condo, there was no high fructose corn syrup sweetened soda to drink or MSG loaded chips to eat, just 100 percent natural fruit juices, pretzels and popcorn for snacks. Maybe even some yogurt and cereals. Not preservative filled, artery clogging crap that she most likely preferred to snack on.

Ali's attorney may have asked her to refute those allegations, but no one cared what she had to say. Not even the allegations about prostitution.

The prosecutor told the jury that even if they didn't believe the pedophile and the jealous babysitter, they had to at least believe Ali's own daughter.

That seemed to be the icing on the cake that put her away. Did anyone care what a pedophile had to say, or some inferior woman who had it against Ali because she was jealous of her youth, beauty and money? Why would the babysitter have it out for her, to say all those horrible things to hurt her?

The truth be told, one night while Ali was over the babysitter's apartment picking up her two children, she had walked there from her condo and had to walk back. It was kind of far. The woman's husband volunteered to walk with her so she wouldn't have to walk alone with her children at night. I mean with it being such a bad neighborhood and all. Yeah right! It was a very nice, quiet development with mostly white yuppies living there.

Go figure...He made a pass at her and she absolutely refused it, then Ali told his wife about it the next day because she thought that the woman was her friend and should know that her beloved husband was a cheating dog like all the others.

Ali wasn't trying to be vindictive.

She was just stupid, to say the least, when it came to trusting others around her. But she still thought that this woman had her best interest at heart when she told Amanda to let Peggy know about the sexual assault and told her to keep the kids safe with her until she got back to them.

WHAT MOST LIKELY GOT ALI convicted was her-own daughter Amanda.

But when Amanda got on the stand to testify, even though she would say the things that would convict her mother, Ali was so proud of her. To see her up on that stand all by herself, looking as adorable as ever. So brave to go up in front of an entire courtroom of familiar and unfamiliar faces. And then, knowing the truth deep down inside, blatantly LIE to them! Wow! That takes a lot of guts, or brainwashing!

There was absolutely no doubt in Ali's mind, that her child had been coached very well for that day. It's absolutely amazing what people will do to get the results that they want at the expense of another human being's life. People can be so nefarious!

Amanda testified that, "every time she told her mother that Fenton was molesting her, her mother would smack her in the face and send her to her room." Talk about payback!

Ali had only smacked Amanda in the face twice in her entire life, if you can believe that. And she never hit her anywhere else on her body ever again, because she felt so guilty about hurting her children, and it wasn't even that hard.

She was not a disciplinary kind of person. She loved to love and loved her children so much that she tried to keep them happy by spoiling them rotten. Not Good! You can see the results.

One time, while she was alone with her children down in Florida, Ali had taken her kids to the local pool. It just happened to be directly across the street from her trailer. It was on a Monday, and she had forgotten that the pool was closed on Mondays.

Amanda saw that the pool was closed, and began screaming at the top of her lungs like someone was trying to kill her. So Ali, who was holding Tyler and trying to stay sane in ninety-degree weather with three irritable children, smacked Amanda across her face.

The other time that Amanda got smacked in her face was when she missed her school bus. She had been horsing around with her brother. Ali had worked all night and was extremely tired and run down and it was a bad reflex. She felt so horrible about it after, that she begged Amanda's forgiveness and then drove her to school. That was it for all the physical abuse. Those were the only two times that her child ever suffered at the hands of her mother. And believe me, Ali lived to regret it!

ALI CHOKED UP WITH EMOTION, seeing her daughter on the stand, and nearly broke down and cried. But not because she knew what was being said, was about to get her sent to prison for a very long time. She knew it wasn't her daughter's fault. Ali believed that Amanda had been coached. For two years, most likely, by her child's psychologist or DYFS to say all those things.

She almost lost her composure and broke down, because no matter what, she was still proud of herself. In her mind, she had created the most beautiful children that ever walked the face of the earth. Her children were her greatest accomplishments in this life. Even if it meant being destroyed by one of them.

But the reality was, she had failed them as their mother. What does the bible say? "A man's foes [shall be] they of his own household." Matthew 10:36

Yeah, I know, her daughter was the poor victim and Ali deserved everything she got for allowing a pedophile to babysit her children, so she could go and live the grand life that she had always wanted to live? As if it were all done intentionally. "Delusions of grandeur?"

And what was the motive for selling her child to this pedophile? Did anyone ever wonder what that was? Everyone has a motive for doing the things they do. Fenton wanted someone to go down with him. That was his motive for testifying against Ali. His daughter wanted Ali to pay for getting her father busted. That was her motive. The babysitter wanted to get Ali into trouble because she was jealous that her husband wanted another woman. Amanda was angry because her mother paid more attention to Tyler than she did her. So what was Ali's motive? She certainly didn't need the money.

She wasn't a desperate drug addict who would sell her own soul for a fix of dope. She was actually trying to make a life with her children finally after all the years of not having them with her. She only had them for a few months before all this happened. She had enrolled her daughter into school. She even refused to live with Fenton when he rented that big house on the water. She had decided that she was going to do everything she could to raise her children alone.

There was NO motive! Three angry people told lies about her and that was enough to convict her for 18 years. She wasn't even there when the crime was committed. "How was that possible?" And that's exactly what Ali kept repeating to her self for many years after it happened.

Ali's children had been doing really well without her in foster care, so she thought. However, Tyler had told her during a visit once that Amanda kept doing things and blaming him for them. He was always getting punished for her dirty deeds. Ali tried to intervene, but no one would listen to her.

She wanted her children to grow up together, but the day she got sentenced, they separated them and never put them together again. They were raised away from each other.

The woman, who had originally taken them into foster care, adored Amanda and believed that Tyler was the problem. But after they sent Tyler to another home, they realized it was really her doing all the crap, so they sent her away as well. Amanda would spend the next ten years going from home to home causing problems everywhere she went. They thought it was because she had been molested, but Amanda caused her brother so much psychological damage with all the negative things she had told him throughout the years, that he actually believes now that his sister is the evil one.

Who knows, Amanda doesn't believe in God. Can people really be born evil?

The state or DYFS or whoever, wanted Ali to have many psychological evaluations, and she complied for the sake of her children. But what she didn't realize was that every evaluation was going to be written in favor of the state, against her. They painted her out to be completely insane, incapable of ever getting her children back and raising them again.

She believes it was mostly because she was a single mother and a stripper. The state also believed she was a prostitute, a drug addict and everything else that one can stereotype someone in her position. But she was none of those things. YET!

Chapter 18

She began her life being born on a bathroom floor in a small apartment on South Clinton Ave. in Trenton New Jersey.

Her father, Gordon C. Durant, delivered her. There were no doctors around or even a midwife to assist him, so he always had a very special bond with his daughter, because he brought her into this world.

After she was born, an ambulance took her and her mother to St. Francis Hospital where they were left on a stretcher in a hallway. Still attached to the umbilical cord, no one would assist them because they were not patients of that hospital.

After nearly six hours with the cord still attached, poison began to set in and the newborn baby began turning multi shades of purple. An oriental male doctor, who was working in the hospital at the time, just happened to be passing by them, and felt sorry for the desperate new mother and her infant and he cut the cord for them.

But because she hadn't been born in the hospital, the staff believed her to be contaminated, refusing to put her in the nursery with the other newborns.

Instead, they cleared out someone's office and put her in there, alone. Clear across the hospital from where they roomed her mother.

From the very beginnings of her life Ali was an outcast and never really felt like she belonged anywhere.

At six weeks old, her parents were driving on a highway and her father decided to make a u-turn that caused the passenger side door to swing open. Her mom had been holding her in her arms wrapped in a light blue baby blanket. There were no laws about the use of car seats or seat belts at that time. When her mother reached out to close the door, Ali flew out of the blanket and onto the highway.

Her baby bonnet had turned black from the road tar. Her parents rushed her to the hospital, where the doctor told them, she had slept through the entire event. He said if she began throwing up, to bring her back to him, because she could have a concussion.

It wasn't until years later when she got her skull fractured by her ex-boyfriend, that someone took a cat scan and an MRI of her head to find that she had a "Huge Arachnoid Cyst" on her left brain. Going from her left frontal lobe to her temporal lobe. She had a big empty space filled with fluid. Caused by an accident they say occurred in the early stages of her life.

She had zero cognitive damage according to tests. They say her brain rewired itself. She was able to function perfectly like any "normal" child. But she was not a normal child. She was hypersensitive to many things that wouldn't affect other children. And she had very bad Asthma that kept her from running around and playing with her other siblings. She was constantly sick, allergic to everything around her. And as she got older, she began to resent the world for being a danger to her health and causing her such physical pain.

Instead of joining other children in play, she kept herself entertained, alone at home, by drawing, coloring and playing the piano. She loved putting puzzles together with her father and playing cards with him.

Her father enjoyed listening to her play the piano for him and she was happy to make him proud of her. She helped in the kitchen all the time and learned to bake cakes and cinnamon buns. Her father loved them.

She began observing the behavior of her siblings, as they got older and disapproved of them. She even resented them at times, wishing she had been an only child. Once again keeping herself isolated from everyone except her parents and a select few friends, who would eventually betray her trust.

Although her dad was a very religious man, her mother was fascinated with the occult. The energies of crystals and the new age concepts fascinated her. Ali enjoyed collecting crystal balls and received her very first one from her mother at twelve years old. Her mother taught her how to scry and how to read Tarot Cards also. She even learned hypnosis and put her mother under once by reading to her from a book.

Her mother thought she had a special gift and taught her daughter how to use it. But her father would fight with his wife, constantly accusing her of tampering with Satan's tools. He even accused her of being demon possessed and tried to exercise the demons from her several times.

Ali just wanted to fit in and keep the peace, so she kept her little "gift" to herself for many years after her father demanded that she keep those demonic things out of his house.

She didn't think he knew what he was talking about. It was a gift from God, not Satan, she thought. But gifts have a way of turning into curses if you don't know how to control them or master them. Or if no one in the mainstream of society accepts them as real. This is where the insanity part comes in.

She was completely honest with the psychologists who evaluated her. And she told them all the things that had happened to her throughout her lifetime. For example: When she was fourteen years old and living in North Carolina with her family, a sixteen year old boy named Clifford Wells, who was friends with her sister Jessica, began telling everyone he knew that he had slept with her. Not a chance! So, one night while her siblings and their friends were hanging out at Jessica's house partying, Ali cornered him in the hall way, put a butcher knife to his neck and threatened to slit his throat for telling lies about her. Her brothers immediately jumped on her and took the knife out of her hand. But before she walked away, she stared into his eyes and told him that he was going to die in a car accident that night. Everyone including Jessica heard her say that to him. Jessica told her that if anything happened to him, she knew Ali had done it and called her an evil witch.

The very next day, the headlines read "High speed chase

ends in wreck". Clifford had left the party, went to a self-paying gas station and filled his tank with gas, taking off without paying for it. The police chased him until he flipped his car six times. Breaking his neck, puncturing his lungs, breaking limbs and needing stitches in his lower lip. He was semi-conscious calling only her name "Alisha".

Jessica grabbed her by the wrist and dragged her to her car. She forced her to drive to the hospital and kiss him on his cheek. She was also forced to tell him that she was sorry. She did it, but with a lot of resistance. He shouldn't have told those lies about her, she said. That wasn't very nice!

And then, there was the time when Jessica's boyfriend Arnold kept hitting her children and Jessica called her, asking her to "Kill him". Ali just laughed. "You've got to be kidding me! And how do you suppose I do that?" she asked "With your Voodoo," Jessica replied

So she focused real hard on his head, and imagined him being struck in the temple with an ice pick. Three days later, he disappeared. Jessica called Ali crying that her Arbe had left her. Ali said, "Well, that's a good thing isn't it?" Then her sister got a call three days later from a hospital that he was in intensive care. Someone had dragged him out of his car in East or South Orange, New Jersey and beat him in the head with a hammer. Wow! What a coincidence, she thought.

What was he doing in the bad section of town for that to happen? He had gone there to buy some crack and have sex with a cheap hooker. The girl must have had him followed afterwards and robbed. What a great guy to have around the children! She thought

Ali told her sister that she felt he was very weak and very close to the shadow. If he went into the shadow he wouldn't be able to come back into this life and would have to move onto the next. So she volunteered to use her gift once again to push him into the shadow.

Jessica insisted that her powers were stronger, and that she was going to wish him to live. Ali said, "Ooh, that sounds like a challenge!" Then her sister backed down and said she loved him and didn't want him to die.

Ali told her not to ever call her again about his abuses if she stayed with him. Eventually they married and she stayed with him for many years to follow. They even had a child together. Arnold never abused the children again after that, at least not to her knowledge.

Whether or not she had anything to do with the stories she told the psychologists, they diagnosed her as having a personality disorder that one psychologist put in his report " would take three to five years of intense psychotherapy before they would even begin to scratch the surface of her deeply embedded problems". They also diagnosed her as Schizotypal with Borderline features. That would be best described on pages 697-698 of the DSM-IV. That's the manual for mental disorders psychologists refer to, in case you're not aware.

In other words, they were saying that she was very eccentric, superstitious, preoccupied with paranormal phenomena, thinking she had special powers to sense events before they happen or was able to read the minds of others which is not exactly accepted by her "subculture".

Here's a clue! If a person is like that, I mean, very superstitious and believing they have some kind of special gift that God gave them, would it make any sense to hurt their own children, since their children are the fruit that they bare in this life to continue their legacy?

Sure it is, to the wacky lunatics who still do virgin sacrifices to the invisible Gods. But not to a woman who feared the God of Abraham, Isaac and Jacob, she may have been a little weird, but it says in the KJV bible, "Gods children are a peculiar people." Deuteronomy 14:2

OF COURSE EVERYONE SHOULD HAVE at least one ghost story to tell in life. This was the one Ali told her psychologists...

It was a nice warm summer night sometime in mid-July of 1990.

Ali had gotten the word that one of her favorite famous

actors was going to be hanging out at the Limelight in New York City that Saturday night. She had been, wanting to meet him for sometime. Planning a night out with a few of her dancer friends from Heartbreakers, she paid for a limo to drive them into the city that night. Everyone was drinking and having a good time except Ali. She just wasn't in the partying mood for whatever reason.

When they finally got to the Limelight from their long drive up the parkway and went inside, Ali saw what appeared to be a group of guys wearing baseball caps, sneakers and jeans standing in the room where she was standing. She said they all knew that she was looking at them and they began laughing at her.

Ali asked her girl friend if she could see them, but her friend said no. They were semi-transparent and Ali knew they were spirits. She got scared thinking of the Exorcist movie and imagined them slamming her up against the wall and pushing her onto the ceiling by using their powers. She began to feel very queasy like she was going to vomit when a guy standing next to her asked her if she was ok. Ali told him she had to get out of there, so he walked her next door to the Hot Tomato and got her a hot cup of tea. Then she told him about the apparitions.

She really thought that she had finally lost her mind but still wanted to go back inside the club to have some fun and hopefully find her actor. After sitting a while in the restaurant, she realized it was only her imagination getting the best of her. But when she got back inside the club, she saw them again as clear as day. She turned and ran outside to sit in the limo and wait for her friends. After sitting a while she got bored and asked the limo driver if he could go inside and get her girlfriends for her. When her friends finally got into the car, one of the ghosts had followed them. He was wearing a long thin brown leather coat and he was crouched down in the doorway as they drove away. Ali freaked out then told everyone in the car that the ghost was now with her. When they got halfway down the road, the spirit turned and went out the closed door to head back to the Limelight. Ali and her friends went to several other places that night, like the Hard Rock Café and Planet Hollywood, but Ali never saw another ghost.

A few days later, she asked Joey to take her back into the city. She told him what had happened and said she refused to let the spirits intimidate her. She wanted to go back to the city during the day while it was light out to overcome her fears. But when they got to the Lincoln Tunnel, she began screaming for Joey to turn around. She had changed her mind and was too afraid to even drive through the tunnel. After that, Ali didn't go back to the city for years insisting that it was full of spirits and not nice ones either.

WITH ALL OF THEIR EVALUATIONS, they should have picked up on the fact that this twenty- five year old, mentally disturbed person, was just as much a victim of that pedophile as her daughter was.

But do you know why they didn't? She believes it's because they weren't suppose to. She had to be punished for not paying attention to her false perceptions. They were twisted and off! She should have known not to allow a man to babysit her children no matter how many other women allowed it. No matter how nice he was to her and her children.

She also believes that going to prison had something to do with her son little Adam Jr. and sending him away with his grandmother that day in Florida. It was her bad karma!

Chapter 19

~~~~~~

There was another incident in her life that some believe was the root of all her disorders. They say early childhood abuse, or trauma in life, causes repressed psychological damage. Perhaps her coping mechanism was triggered by what happened to her when she had just turned sweet sixteen.

She had moved to the Pocono Mountains with her family after leaving Jacksonville, North Carolina and the ninth grade. She was going to Mt. Pocono High with her brothers Pete, and Chris, who had met two cousins, Loni Walker and Lana Walker. Pete began dating Loni who he met in school and Chris followed by dating Lana soon after. Loni's, mother, Nicole, became close friends with Ali's, mother Delse. Loni had an older brother who had just come to live with them from Los Lobos, California. His name was Henry Robert Walker, but everyone called him Rob. He was nineteen years old, six foot four, with mysterious blue eyes and thick, straight, dark brown hair that he kept parted in the middle. He had a very cool style that made him seem different from all the other guys at the mountain high school.

Ali's two brothers and their girlfriends thought that it would be fun if she dated him. There would be an even greater family connection. So when Ali met Rob at a local party, they began dating almost immediately. She found him very attractive and yet, he reminded her of Lurch from the Addams Family in some odd way.

She resonated with the oddness of the characters on those shows "The Munster's and the Addams Family" because she always felt like she was the odd one out, like Marilyn Munster. Every time she would bring a "Normal" guy home, her brothers would scare him away. She had five of them and three sisters too. She was exactly in the middle and was the same age as Pete.

Pete, Bob and Andrew weren't her biological brother's, they were actually her first cousins who got adopted by her parents when she was just six years old.

Her mother's only brother Robert and his wife Brenda had been killed in a car accident while Christmas shopping one year. They lived in New Hampshire at the time. No one wanted their three boys so Ali's dad Gordon felt obligated to take them in.

Jessica was actually her half sister and so was Louise. The only children her parents had together were Chris, Alisha, Bart and Claire in that order. Pete was the same age as her when they met at six years old and he was her favorite brother growing up. He was actually murdered later in life at the age of thirty-three, leaving behind a wife and daughter.

Only two weeks after they had begun seeing each other, he began physically abusing her. For no reason, he would just, out of the blue, start pushing her around and hitting on her.

She had been working at the Pocono Race track with her mother, and had to show up for work several times with a busted lip and a black eye. She was too embarrassed to tell anyone what had happened, but they all knew.

One woman even advised her to get out of the relationship and have him arrested. But Ali didn't listen. She found herself making excuses for him. The truth was, she was afraid to get out and was still oddly attracted to him.

Ali didn't understand abuse at the time and how it worked. She thought that he would stop. Two weeks after the abuse began, he told her that he wanted to marry her and if she didn't marry him, he would kill her. She just wanted everyone to be happy, herself included. But her dad had just left her mother in the Pocono's, and moved back to Trenton after he had suspected his wife of having another affair with a guy who owned a local pub.

Her brothers spent most of their days drinking and smoking pot and hanging around the house while their mother worked to support them all.

Ali thought that if she married this guy, he would be happy because he was getting what he wanted. Her brothers would be happy because she would be officially bonding the two families together forever.

She convinced her mother to sign permission for her to get married. It was the law for anyone under eighteen to get written marital permission from a guardian. Ali's mother usually went along with anything her children wanted to do or did, mostly trying to fit in or stay friends with them. It was important for her to be liked. Ali's father was the complete opposite. He didn't care who liked him and was very blunt with letting anyone know when he disapproved of them or bad behavior. He was the strict one. Ali admired his strength and courage of conviction. She had no respect for weak people who just floated along like a leaf on the river of time. She wanted to be like her father, the grounded, solid oak tree in the forest of human potential. Unfortunately even oak trees are vulnerable to the savage of human nature.

Chapter 20

So...On June 12th, 1981 in Scranton, Pennsylvania, Alisha and Henry Robert Walker stood before the Justice of the Peace and exchanged their vows of marriage.

She was wearing a blue flowered sundress with blue flip-flops, and he was wearing an unbuttoned, blue and black flannel shirt, with a black T-shirt underneath, blue jeans and biker boots, with a chain hanging from his wallet tucked into his back right pocket.

The JP recited Psalms 23 at some point during the ceremony. And it was when he spoke the words "Yea though I walk through the valley of the shadow of death, I will fear no evil" that Ali felt like she was marrying Satan Himself.

So why didn't she run? Why didn't she stop and say NO?

Because a part of her was flattered that someone wanted to marry her. Her mother had once told her that she was such a "Bitch" she was going to die an old maid; that no one would ever want to marry her.

But why was she a bitch? Was it because she had no respect for her mother after witnessing her having an affair with someone less worthy, while her faithful, hard working father was at work? Or maybe it was because she had a real hard time accepting the fact that her weak demoralized mother actually had an affair with her own daughter's husband, Ali's older sister, knowing she had two grand children from him. Jessica may have forgiven her, but that sort of behavior was unforgivable to Ali.

She was actually the one who had told her father about the

first affair. She loved and respected him with all of her heart and felt he didn't deserve the injustice being inflicted upon him behind his back? That's the reason her father had sold their beautiful house, that he had built just for his family and divorced her mother.

Was it also her fault that her siblings had turned out to be a bunch of lazy, alcoholic, uneducated losers? And that's exactly how Ali had felt about them.

She had always dreamed of her father giving her away at her big white wedding to the perfect man. But no one her father would approve of was going to marry a woman who had a family as disappointing as hers.

Another huge factor was that she was just simply afraid to say no. She feared retaliation with no one to protect her.

She was so humiliated by her weakness to give into this man, that she didn't even let her father know she had gotten married. Two weeks went by before her brother Bart finally let him know. He was so saddened and disappointed that she hadn't let him be there, but she didn't want him to yell at her or to know how weak she had been, to allow someone like this monster to bully her into such a commitment. The only thing keeping that marriage binding was the FEAR, not the love.

On their wedding night, Rob had drunk an entire fifth of Jack Daniel's Whiskey and beat her like she had never been beaten before.

Her mom had to go to work after the wedding was over. And while the rest of her siblings drank beer and whiskey all night, she sipped on a small glass of Tia Maria coffee liquor (her favorite). After a few hours of partying, Rob had followed her into her mother's bedroom and pushed her onto the bed, face down. He began punching her in the back of her head. Chris walked in and witnessed him on top of her, and instead of coming to her rescue, he yelled, "Yeah man, fuck her up! Show her whose boss!"

Ali would never forgive her brother for that night. Her other brother Pete went to investigate and tried to get him to stop, yelling for him to get off of her, but Rob got up and punched him in the face, causing him to just walk away saying "Fuck that shit, I'm not getting involved." Pete was a very small, timid guy, but Chris was six feet tall and strong enough to hurt anyone. He just happened to like Rob more than his own sister.

No one even thought to call the police. When Rob had gotten off of her to hit Pete, she was able to get up off the bed. He then picked up a wooden speaker, sitting on the dresser connected to her mother's stereo, and he threw it in her face, just missing her eye. The corner of the speaker hit her with such force, that it literally knocked her out.

The next thing she knew, she was hanging over his shoulder watching droplets of her blood slowly make a path across the living room floor. As it dripped onto the carpet, he carried her out the front door.

Claire was sitting in her boyfriend Kevin's white Jeep in the driveway. As Rob carried her past them, Ali began crying for her little sister to save her. No one moved as he continued to walk with her down the dark, unpaved, isolated country road, with no street lights to light the way, only spooky quiet moonlight and trees as far as the eye could see.

He gently put her down in front of him. They were standing in the middle of the dark road with no one around to hear him. When his eyes met hers, she could see that he was possessed with an evil spirit. Perhaps the spirit that sometimes possesses people when they drink hard whiskey. But it wasn't just the whiskey making him crazy. He was truly insane. Evil! Pure evil permeated from his entire being. Then he said to her in a calm voice "I'm going to kill you and put your body out into the woods where no one is ever going to find you." And he meant it!

She just stood there frozen, afraid to say a single word that might set him off to fulfill his dark, twisted fantasy. She prayed silently in her mind to the God in heaven to keep her safe and to protect her from the evil that was now standing right in front of her, threatening her life. "In the name of God, I command you to leave me alone!" she thought to herself. Was this how she was going to die? Being murdered at sixteen by her insane, evil husband who had forced her into marriage? We come into this world alone and we leave it alone. All alone!

Suddenly, the Jeep began backing out of the driveway. She could see the headlights from a distance. Kevin and Claire began driving towards them.

There were deep drainage ditches on the side of the road next to where they were standing, and Rob grabbed her by her shoulders, tossing her into the ditch, full of sticker bushes that cut her arms and legs and made her bleed. He jumped on top of her and held his hand over her mouth so she couldn't scream. But as soon as she saw the white Jeep, right next to where she was lying, she bit his hand and began kicking and screaming to let them know where she was.

Kevin stopped, and Claire yelled "Come on Rob, it's your wedding night and you're missing the party. Come back with us and have some more fun". So Rob got off of her, pulling her to her feet. He yanked her out of the ditch and told her to get into the truck, which was still running.

It just so happened that her mom was getting home at that precise moment and drove right next to them to check on everyone. Ali saw her mother and ran to her car, jumping into the front seat. Sliding over to her, practically jumping on top of her, wanting protection from the demon that was trying to kill her. Rob jumped into the car next to Ali as she screamed and cried for him to get away. Then he said in a calm voice, "Honestly Mrs. Durant, I didn't touch her, she fell".

They all went back to the house and tried to resolve the situation. No cops were ever called, no one was arrested and she didn't die that night.

He would keep her prisoner for the next few months doing things to her that she would have nightmares about for the rest of her life.

He got her on a bed one day and appeared to be in a trance when he began choking her to death. Right before she went unconscious, his sister came into the room and snapped him out of it.

She couldn't even go to the bathroom without him following her. He would wake up in the middle of the night, punch her in the face while she slept and go back to sleep as if nothing ever happened. Then he claimed he didn't remember a thing when he woke up. She truly believed he was demon possessed.

He told her once that he was going to take a nap and said not to go anywhere. They had been watching TV in her bedroom. She got hungry and left the room to make some Kraft Macaroni and Cheese while he slept.

She returned to the bedroom after cooking and continued watching TV next to him while she ate. He woke to find her eating and said, "I thought I told you not to go anywhere". She replied " I only went into the kitchen to make something to eat." she even asked him if he wanted some, to be polite. That was all it took for him to flip out and beat her up again.

What an asshole! She thought. He got off on the control. He always apologized and constantly told her how much he loved her after the abuse was over.

Two weeks after they were married, Rob took her to Ranton, Vermont to live on a dairy farm with him and his father's family. His half brother had come to visit and drove back with them. Rob's father had remarried and had several other children with another woman. They were all just a little older than Ali was.

Robs other family owned a dairy farm right outside of the quaint little town of Ranton. It was just about six miles away from the town itself. They stayed at Robs older sisters house across from the farm. Her name was Sharon and she had a baby nine months old named Scotty Jr. with her husband.

All the men, including Rob, got up every morning at 5:30 AM to milk the cows and work the farm. It was a fairly large farm with at least sixty cows, maybe even more. Everyone there smoked Marijuana except her. They secretly grew it on their farm. Sharon had taken Ali into town and helped her get a job at a Ralph Lauren Polo Shirt factory, where she did the inventory for the shirts.

She worked alone in a quiet office all day enjoying her sanctuary and peace of mind. She worked as many hours over time as she was allowed, and every chance she got, because she didn't want to go back to her nemesis. They had to sleep together on a couch in Sharon's living room at night and Ali cringed at the thought of having to be so close to him.

Rob was on his best behavior with her for a short time because his other family wouldn't tolerate him abusing his young teenage wife. But that didn't last long before his true colors began showing again. When he thought no one was looking, he would lash out at her. Usually in the middle of the night or when they would take walks together on the long country roads.

Niche once said "What doesn't kill you will make you stronger." Whatever!

Rob finally went to jail for aggravated assault on another person. He only spent six months behind bars on an eighteen-month sentence. But it was just enough time for Ali to break the bond with him and move on. She left Vermont on a bus and moved to Waldwick, New Jersey with her family. She was never with him again and eventually got the marriage annulled.

While Rob was in jail, he wrote to her nearly everyday expressing his love for her. He told her he had tattooed her name on his body in ten different places. He was truly obsessed with her! She actually only read a few of the many letters that he wrote though, because every time she tried to read one, that dark, suffocating feeling of evil would fill her mind with pure unfiltered FEAR.

She would keep his last name for a while to remind her of what marriage meant to her. Bondage, torture, and pain! His name also reminded her of freedom. The strength, courage and knowledge that she developed to never again allow her self to be the victim of a controlling freak. If anyone even threatened to hurt her again, she would call the police immediately and have them arrested.

Satan would get her in other ways now. And someone else would come into her life to finish destroying her spirit. And that man was Amanda's father, who she met at a trade school while her husband, was in jail.

Was it adultery in the eyes of God? I guess not if she was never with him again. But who knows!

Chapter 21

Ali was just starting to get her life back on track. Her father had given her a little brown Hornet Station wagon to drive so she could get herself to school. She had completed a state funded program called CEFA where she actually got a paycheck every other week for studying to get her GED. As soon as she finished that program and got her GED from the Lexington Community College, she entered another one where she was taught office skills, typing, filing, etc.

She had also taken the Arms Forces test and passed it with high scores to enroll into the Army. She was scheduled to go into boot camp on October 15th, 1982.

She imagined herself studying for a degree while traveling the world. She loved learning new things. Anything, that, anyone else could teach her. She was free from the physical abuse and was now hoping to find a nice boyfriend to share her life with, who was more sensitive in nature and perhaps more romantic.

She should have learned her lesson with guys by then and stayed away from them. Maybe she would have become a very successful career woman. But she was always searching for that special feeling. That, take my breath away, love at first sight kind of feeling. And for some reason, it was never with a clean cut, wealthy, successful business type man. She always gravitated to the hopeless, lost, rebels that stood out from the norm, who had no money to make even their own dreams come true. The type of guys that most likely fit into her dysfunctional family.

ONE DAY, SOMETIME IN MAY of 1982, when she stepped outside on her break at the clerical program, that's when they found each other. She believed in love at first sight and he was someone she felt she would love for the rest of her life.

His name was David, but everyone called him "Trippin Hippie" or just "Hippie." He was sitting in his little blue Capri sports car with license plates that read 321-STN. He was just nineteen years old and was wearing cut off jean shorts that showed off his thin, shapely, hairy legs and a dark gray Harley Davidson T-shirt. He had a rose tattoo on his left cheek just below his eye and a girls name tattooed on his upper arm. He had long straight dark brown hair that he hid under a leather Harley cap and the sexiest brown eyes. But he also had the most beautiful lips, the whitest teeth and the sweetest smile, she thought. He smoked Kool cigarettes and tore the filters off before he lit them. He carried with him a leather bound book filled with his own poetry. He was a poet and a very good one, she thought.

She learned to dress for success in her programs, looking professional by wearing beautiful dresses and high-heeled shoes that showed off her womanly shape. She had the scent of sweet flowers and never had a problem catching the eye of the opposite sex. She had a lot of class and style, but her taste in men didn't match her image. She adored the bohemian, creative artist type or the blue-collar worker.

As soon as they met, they fell in love. For the next three weeks they would spend countless hours together just gazing into each other's eyes, passionately kissing and holding, caressing and touching. It was all that she had dreamed about for years.

Where did this Adonis come from? He had been adopted by an Italian couple who. They had gone to an orphanage in Italy to find him when he was an infant.

David was in a metal shop program in the back of the school in another building and everyday they would meet on their lunch break.

There was a small Sabrett hotdog wagon always parked on

the side of the road near the school, and quite often, the two lovers, hand in hand, would walk to get a hotdog from the vendor, with chili, mustard and onions.

Then one day, Ali went out to meet him on her break and found, sitting in the passenger side of his car, a very thin, beautiful Irish girl with the thickest, longest brownish blonde hair she had ever seen and very pretty green eyes. The girl was talking with him and wearing his Harley cap. Her name was Lisa, not the same name tattooed on his arm either.

Ali had just given him, that very morning, a drawing she had spent eight hours working on the night before. It was of a man holding a lantern out over a mountain that she had copied from one of the Led Zeppelin albums. She noticed it torn into a hundred pieces and scattered in the parking lot next to his car.

She knew that Lisa had done it out of jealousy, but why? Who was this girl that just showed up out of the blue three weeks after David had fallen in love with her? Go figure! It was his girlfriend, whom he had been living with for the past eleven months and cheating on with her. What an asshole she thought.

She was so hurt. She couldn't believe how he could have played her like that. He seemed so real, so honest and gentle and kind.

Ali suddenly became furious and told him that they were over. He begged her right in front of Lisa not to go. She said, "Right now, who do you love, her or me? Pick one!" He told her that he loved her. So she got into his car and they drove out of the parking lot, leaving his ex-lover behind.

Soon after he had declared his love for her, they moved into an efficiency apartment at the Sleepy Hollow cabins in Brandon. They lived there together for the next several months.

After only two months of living together, David had disappeared all night and Ali stayed up worrying about him. He had never done that to her before. He told her he had spent the night at his friend Martin's. Coincidentally, about two weeks later, she had picked up a couple girls hitch hiking, and they told her about David making love to their friend, and then leaving her early the next morning, at Martin's house, the same night he had disappeared from Ali.

David never physically abused her, but what he did for the next two years that they spent together, was far worse to her then any beatings. He lied to and cheated on her constantly. He got her pregnant two months before she was scheduled to go into the military and begged her to stay and have their "Love Child", then left her when she was in her sixth month. He taught her all about the cons of men and their hidden agendas while he cried to her endlessly, begging her forgiveness, time and time again, only to go out the very next day and repeat his behavior. She always found sympathy to forgive him, but subconsciously began to resent him for it.

Her father had even given David hundreds of dollars not to return, when he left her pregnant, but three days after Amanda was born, he had been released from the county jail and showed up at her house wanting to get back together with her. Ali took him back for the baby's sake.

He was always in trouble with the law, for stupid things like selling fake drugs on the beach. He couldn't even help him self, he lied to everyone, all the time about everything. Robbing old people by telling them he was a construction man, so they would give him money to do a job and then he wouldn't complete it or do it right.

She watched him frame a house one day in a retirement village, and when he was finished, she asked him where the doors and windows were. He said he was going to cut them out after. He had framed the entire house with no openings for doors or windows. He had no clue how to do his job. Maybe he meant well, but he was absolutely stupid. She thought he had a problem being a pathological liar also. She made excuses for his behavior. "It's not his fault; he's mentally disturbed."

One day she had gotten invited to a party where a few of her friends were going to be hanging out. She wanted him to come with her, but there was going to be a guy there who wanted to kick David's ass for screwing his wife while he was in jail. Nice guys huh? Her friends told her they would protect him if he went.

When they got to the party, the guy asked him to step outside, but he refused. So he jumped him right in the house. David just sat there not even trying to defend himself. Some of Ali's friend's pulled the guy off of him and dragged him outside, forcing him to leave the party.

She was so humiliated that she had a boyfriend who was such a wimp. He had the balls to screw a man's wife, but not any to defend him self?

What a creep! She thought

Ali began drinking beer excessively out of disgust, to the point of being extremely intoxicated. When they got home later that evening, she told David that she hated him so much, she could kill him. So he handed his drunk, angry girlfriend a steak knife out of the kitchen drawer and said, "Go ahead!"

She stuck the knife deep into his upper thigh just two inches from his dirty, uncircumcised pisser. Blood instantly filled his pant leg. She fell to the floor laughing hysterically at the moron, for daring her to do something that she had been Desiring to do for such a long time.

He had to go to the hospital to get a few stitches, but for the most part, he wasn't hurt that bad, it could have been much worse. She was only trying to make a statement and put some fear into him that she wasn't going to put up with his shit any more.

Ali gave him fare warning that she couldn't take it any longer and was going to kill him if he didn't leave her. She knew she was at her breaking point. For her to find pleasure in stabbing another human being, their relationship was in serious trouble.

But then, he took her to a bar in Sandy Hook to party a couple weeks later. He became very seductive and romantic with her. Holding her, kissing her and slow dancing with her. She was only trying to have a good time as a teenager, while her parents babysat Amanda.

He handed her a matchbook and asked her to open it. On

the inside cover were words he had written in pen "Will you marry me?" Young love is so predictable isn't it? Of course she said yes. It was after a few good drinks no doubt.

Afterwards, they went back to their apartment and made mad passionate love to each other and she fell asleep in his arms.

The next morning, he awakened to tell her he was going to make her breakfast in bed, but he had to go to the Krauser's at the end of their street to get some bacon and eggs. He told her not to get up, that he'd be right back.

Two hours later she realized he wasn't coming back, so she got herself dressed, to go over to her parents house to get their daughter. Five days later, he showed up with another girl's car.

She told him he had until midnight, that night, to return the car or she was moving back home with her parents. He never returned. Two weeks later, she got wind from one of her friends that he was going back to their apartment to get his belongings.

Ali decided to throw a fair well party for the father of her baby girl. Amanda was now eight months old and she was holding her in her arms when he showed up at their vacated apartment for his clothes.

He brought back with him, a beautiful, young, sexy brunette who just happened to be the owner of the car he had been driving. It was the first time she had actually seen him with another female and it went beyond jealousy to traumatic pain.

There was nothing she could say or do to change what was about to happen. He had found someone else to replace her. It was a relationship that should have ended long before she stabbed him. Ali just kissed the girl on the cheek and said "Good-luck! You're going to need it".

She knew his ways, and he wasn't going to be faithful or honest to anyone, not even the raving beauty he flaunted in her face. So while she held their love child in her arms, she watched him walk out of her life forever, with another woman.

She was so traumatized from the abandonment, that she felt herself go completely numb inside. An emotional breakdown, that would last for the next several years that followed. The pain of rejection and abandonment had been so severe, that she just stopped feeling.

Co-dependency is a disorder that many people suffer with every single day. They would rather put up with physical or emotional abuse than be alone. They feel that they are nothing or no one without someone with them to love or be loved by. They are so desperate to have someone love them, they are willing to take a beating or deal with the cheating and lying of their "significant other."

Becoming independent is learned behavior. Sometimes people get pushed to the brink of murder to stop the pain, instead of just walking away and calling it quits. It's like any other addiction or drug that can and will eventually destroy you if you don't get it under control.

FOUR MONTHS LATER, MARTIN WOULD show up at her house with Adam. He was extremely strong yet very quiet and gentle. All of her friends feared him. And yet, he was like a ferocious lion that defended her honor and kept her safe for the next four years, giving her two more children to love. He thought of Amanda as his own and cared deeply for her.

But where the hell was he, when Ali needed him to take care of Fenton for molesting her child?

Chapter 22

There was absolutely no privacy any longer. Officers were constantly coming off the elevator with other prisoners. They would walk right by the huge glass window that showed the entire room and the woman sitting on the mattress. Everyone had to look inside to see who was in there out of curiosity if for no other reason.

When she had to use the toilet, she had to accept that someone was going to pass by her and see her doing her business. It was extremely humiliating for her to say the least, but why should she care, she was dead anyway. It wasn't her they saw, it was the body she was trapped in that they watched, both the men and the women.

The only sounds in her cell were that of the metal doors clanging shut behind the prisoners or when the shifts changed.

A person can adjust to any situation, no matter how traumatic it may be. Think of the prisoners in the concentration camps during the Holocaust. They had to endure far worse tortures than imaginable. And yes, Ali compared her self to those helpless victims of war. She was absolutely being tortured in her mind. She believed that the heat was deliberately turned off in her cell for that reason and no blankets given to warm her.

No one was going to feel sorry for the convicted felon, especially the officers in charge. They got off on the power! Not all of them, but one she recalled in particular. A big black woman they called "Candy". She had a very pretty face colored with makeup and beautiful dread lock hair extensions. She was a real "Bitch" in all the sense of the word. Not to mention that she was very overweight and most likely enjoyed the cold air.

Ms. Durant was a petite one hundred four pounds, five foot four blonde who had dyed her hair brown for the trial so hopefully no one would recognize her. She had no body fat to keep her warm. Surprisingly though she never caught pneumonia.

She was eventually moved into the girls section of the county jail and put into a cell close to the officers desk where they could keep an eye on her...the cell they used for suicide watch. She finally flipped out and began tearing the paper gowns from her body, screaming and crying. She just didn't want anything touching her. Everything around her felt filthy and suffocating.

She curled up naked into fetal position on the cold, empty mattress and symbolically died. Shedding all of the sin, all of the ungodly negative world energies that she had accumulated in her life, and let them all go into the eternal abyss, not realizing at that moment she was being reborn into a new person, one much stronger with more patience and understanding of the world, someone not afraid of her destiny.

Romans 12:2- "And be not conformed to this world: but be ye transformed by the renewing of your mind, that ye may prove what [is] that good, and acceptable, and perfect, will of God."

The sheriff's officers saw her doing this and came running. They gathered around her and the next thing she knew, a needle was being stuck into her. And then, with the assistance of the officers in their white shirts and gold badges, She was gently put down like a euthanized dog and covered in a wool blanket, where she slept for what seemed to her like several days.

WHEN SHE AWAKENED, SHE WAS curious of her surroundings and slowly came out of her shell. She talked with the other inmates and told them what had happened to her. She spent the next six months awaiting her sentence. She couldn't be sentenced until she had another psyche evaluation. Only this one was going to be at an adult diagnostic treatment facility called Avenel, where they kept all the felony sex offenders in New Jersey. Her appointment would be four months from the time of her conviction.

She could have been released on bail again to await her sentencing, but she didn't want to prolong the agony. She accepted her fate and stayed in jail to adjust to her new world.

It was the first time in her entire life that she thought people could understand and empathize with her pain. She felt that they could now see what she had been feeling for so long. They could see the torture of her soul because she was locked behind bars. But she was no more imprisoned there than she had been in her mind prior to being locked up. Jail was only the visual of her long, suffering, imprisonment that she had dealt with for many years on her own, on the outside. She was imprisoned with her own desires to find the perfect soul mate, so she could live "Happily Ever After."

If she failed the evaluation, she would be sentenced under Avenel's rules and classified as a repetitive sex offender. She most likely wouldn't get out until they felt she was no longer a threat to society. This could take longer than the sentence under the prison rules.

In other words, they wanted to know if she was going to be a repetitive offender. How to hell can someone be a repetitive offender when they didn't do it in the first place? She wondered.

She always tried to make the best of a bad situation. She had faith that everything happened for a reason and that there must be some grand reason for her being there that was beyond her understanding.

She decided to take advantage of the available options. If she couldn't work, she would study to get a degree. She got some of her friends, on the outside, to pay for correspondence college courses from Thomas Edison College. She took General Earth Science and American History 1. How exciting it was to finally be taking college courses! That's the only reason she got her GED years before; she had wanted a college education.

She also spent much of her time coloring cloth hankies and reading books. She wrote letters occasionally but she hated it, thinking it was a waste of time to communicate with others on the outside, unless she needed something, or if they had news of her children.

She was on the inside now and found herself mentally detached from the outside world. She could care less what was going on out there. She wanted to live inside her head now, to fill it with knowledge she had never acquired before, and forget about all the people who had read those scandalous things about her.

SHE KEPT IN TOUCH WITH Arnold, the bass player from the New Jersey rock band.

She had actually spent her last night in the free world at his beautiful mansion with him. She had gone over there to show him all the news paper articles about her from the past week, and how she was plastered all over the front pages everyday, as if she were someone infamously important. He said, "Wow, Ali, you're going to jail tomorrow for a long time." She agreed. He was so naively sweet.

He ran around the house, searching for things that he thought she might need there, a radio and headphones, a small TV and a few other things. Ali just laughed! She knew that there was nothing allowed into the jail like that. Books had to be mailed directly from the stores, and everything else purchased from commissary. She just wanted to be with her friend, who had in his own way, made it in this life. She knew he had his problems, but he turned out to be a great friend to her. She loved him very much and felt bad for him that he had everything and yet he had nothing that would make him truly happy.

He wrote to her while on tour for the 'Keeping A Promise" album and even sent her a photo of himself so she could remember what he looked like after she had been in jail for a while.

Chapter 23

～～～～～～～～～～～～～～～～～～～～

She had finally been called to take the trip to Avenel for her evaluation. Shacked and handcuffed in her blue county uniform, Ali was escorted by two officers to an office inside the building that housed sex offenders. One of the male psychologists assisted her in a six-hour evaluation.

He asked her a slew of questions that really freaked her out. She felt that even the psychologist himself seemed to be possessed by some sick, twisted spirit of perversion. The entire place reeked of evil, carnal lust and perversion. There were no other words to describe it. The energies were worst there than they were at the topless bar in Florida years before, when she had gotten on stage for the first time.

There is nothing in this world that is more evil, than a man molesting a child or killing one after, and that entire place was filled with those kinds of men. Sick, twisted, evil creatures that should have been executed for their crimes, but were able to be kept alive for possible release later, to do it all again somewhere else.

The Megan's Law hadn't been in affect at that time. That's the law that forces sex offenders to register with the police departments, so they can keep track of their whereabouts. Thank God it came a couple years later. It was well overdue!

She believes that it's Michael the Arch Angel who came to protect the children, by allowing that law to get passed. It's also spooky that her niece, whose name is Megan, was one of the children, he had confessed to molesting along with Amanda.

Daniel 12:1- "And at that time shall Michael stand up, the

great prince which standeth for the children of thy people: and there shall be a time of trouble, such as never was since there was a nation [even] to that same time: and at that time thy people shall be delivered, every one that shall be found written in the book."

THE PSYCHOLOGIST ASKED HER TO draw a house. She drew a church with a cross on the top. He asked her to draw herself. She drew a woman covered in a robe from head to toe, kneeling down in a praying position.

All of his sexually, demeaning questions, would be answered by her as if they were answered by a Holy Nun who had committed her life to God The Father. She imagined that she was Katharina Von Bora again, the wife of Martin Luther. She knew that God was the only one who could protect her from the demonic forces that surrounded her in that place. The same dark forces that caused her to be singled out, of all the mothers whose children had been molested over the years by Fenton Noor, to have to endure the humiliation of being accused with him as an accomplice to his crime.

Surprisingly, she passed the exam, to be sentenced as a common sex offender criminal and not the overly perverted, sick, disturbed one, who got off on the molestation of little children. But others wouldn't see it that way. Any "Sex Offender" is a child molester, no matter what the truth is.

THEN THE TIME FINALLY CAME for sentencing...

Ali said to her self before she went into the courtroom, "Remember that man Lies! No matter how much time the judge may give you, it's a lie! You will get out when God feels that it's time. People have to pay for their sins and mistakes. You have to go through the fire to be cleansed. It's the only way".

And then, while standing before the great arbiter, she was sentenced to eighteen years in maximum security at the Edna Mahon Correctional Facility for Women in Clinton, New Jersey.

As soon as she heard those words, she looked up to the ceiling and silently asked God, "Is it really going to take that long?" She thought about Franc and how she wasn't going to be marrying him in 1994. She was wrong about her vision. What else had she been wrong about, she wondered.

Ali had spoken to Holly right after her sentencing. Holly told her that she had a wonderful surprise for her. Then she played a song into the phone that Franc had written and recorded during her incarceration. He spoke of a woman who had knocked at his door with the face of an angel. They had fallen in love and then she went away. He said that he was hurt by love because he would never be able to find another girl the same color eyes and features of her face. Then, Ali heard a woman crying out for him to "come find my love." Ali's heart nearly stopped beating from the pain it hurt so much. She felt that the voice crying out should have been her own on that recording. He should have recorded her voice for that song. She broke down and cried with sadness but then her feelings turned to rage. How could he! He has NO honor! She screamed into the phone. That's my song! He should have used me to complete it.

When she calmed down, she realized how impossible that would have been.

SHE WAS SHIPPED OUT A week before she was able to take her finals on the college courses, so she never got the credits for them. Her General Earth Science professor had written on her returned thesis, that in his many years of teaching, he had never before read such an incredibly well thought-out paper. She received an A plus on it.

Some of the other female inmates that she had shared space with also read her paper and commented that it was done in an Ali style, whatever that meant.

Chapter 24

On August 16, 1993, Alisha Durant was transported to the only female prison in the state of New Jersey.

She would be identified as number 15581. She would be given an ID to wear on her khaki uniform at all times and would be strip searched, "Turn around, squat and cough. Lift your feet, open your mouth and stick out your tongue!" She had to sleep in a room with sixty bunks and shower with a group of other female inmates until processing was completed. About seventy five percent of the women were bisexual or gay and many of them were HIV positive.

She would cling to her bible as if it were her only shield to protect herself from the unknown dark forces that still appeared to be all around her. She wasn't afraid of any of the other women at all. What she feared most was going into lockdown for doing something that was against the rules, and getting a charge that would take away her chances of ever getting out. If she was going to play this game, she wanted a spotless record.

She spent her time coloring, writing and studying the bible. She didn't need the emotional bonding of other females or the co-dependency that she observed so often around her. She found it disturbing to witness women desperately clinging to other women that they just met, believing themselves to be "In love" with that person until the other person was transferred out of the unit.

Then, within a day or two, that same person would find

themselves desperately "In love" with another person in the unit who would pay attention to them.

Ali thought that they were totally emotionally disturbed. She didn't have time for any sort of warped relationship with anyone. She was polite and friendly, but distant and forthright.

Women had always been the competition for her, nothing more. If she couldn't be with the one she loved, she would NOT love the one she's with. They were all females and not her type at all to be attracted to sexually. She was so disgusted with the world by then that she wanted nothing to do with anyone still in it and that included the inmates.

After weeks in the processing unit, she was sent to the maximum security building "Z Cottage." The unit that had the reputation of housing the "crazy ones."

She spent more time in two other dorms with thirteen bunks and then was finally put into her own room where she would spend the next four years.

Her room had a real wooden door with a small window at eye level. It had a real wooden dresser painted yellow and a picture window where she could see out at the yard and beyond the razor wire fences at the beautiful, tranquil, serene rolling hills of North Jersey.

For the first time in years, she would feel safe. Safe when she was locked in at night. Ali knew that no one was going to break in and hurt her. When she lived alone, she would always sleep with a sharp dagger under her pillow in fear of a break in.

She no longer had to worry about car payments and car insurance, rent, phone bills or any other necessities that forced her into the world of stripping, a world that caused her so much stress. She could finally rest in peace. Dead to the outside, she would spend her time in the pretend art studio that she always dreamed of having.

Ok, so there were some disadvantages in this studio. No real paints were allowed in, like oils or acrylics, but it would have to do.

She decided that she was not put into prison to protect society from her, she was put into a sanctuary to protect her from the corrupt, perverted, evil, deceiving world that had nearly cost her, her life and had stolen away her children. She would spend the next few years cleansing her mind and her soul of the crap that she had seen or done to pollute it.

She couldn't eat the food that was served. It was too heavy and she'd throw it up, so she lived on crackers and apple juice that she purchased from commissary for the next three years. Once in a while she would splurge and buy some pretzels or a sprite. But that was rare. She ate only the egg whites when they served hard-boiled eggs in the kitchen, and the bananas. Only for the protein and the potassium.

Everyday, she would go out to the yard and walk the circle. Twenty-two laps were equivalent to one mile. She would try to walk five miles every chance she got. She had watched many women, who had come into the prison thin and attractive, gain fifty or more pounds within six months of being there, just by eating out of boredom and not exercising, but Ali stayed the same. She was not going to use prison as an excuse to let herself go. She held onto the belief that someday she would be free again to be with her true love. She imagined them living in a big house with all of her children and one more. She would give him one of his own as a gift for accepting her other children into his life.

ALI NEVER STOPPED THINKING ABOUT Franc. He was in her thoughts every moment of everyday. She would look out to the rolling hills and imagine him in his military uniform coming out from behind the tree's to meet her.

She had taken the photograph of their first kiss at Count Basie Theater and weaved it into a tapestry that she sent to a friend who entered it into the largest needlepoint exhibition in America. The competition was held annually at some mansion in Virginia. Ali's needlepoint tapestry called "First Kiss" took first place among five thousand entries that year.

Most of the time, she hated getting letters. It only meant

someone was invading her space from the outside and making her feel obligated to take the time to write him or her back. She only wanted to hear from Franc who never wrote to her, but he once sent her a piano keyboard and a sterling silver cross necklace. Every time she tried to play his keyboard she would envision the white piano and Rylan and get this overwhelming desire to slit her wrists. So she put it under her metal cot and left it there for the remainder of her stay.

Whenever she thought about her children, the thought of suicide followed. She intentionally blocked them from her mind as much as she could for that reason.

She had decided that she was on a mission to create and she crocheted twenty-one afghan's, did thirty-five expensive cross-stitches, ten extremely large original needlepoint tapestries and drew hundreds of pastel drawings that she sent to Holly to hold for her until her release. Most of the tapestries and drawings were of Franc and Ali wanted him to see them to know that she was still in love with him

She sent her daughter a beautiful cross-stitch of an angel that took her weeks to complete and sent her son's crocheted Afghans.

The package sergeant let a lot of her art supplies in. She was really lucky. She had a few friends on the outside with money who, cared about her. Her first cousin, Jacob, was the captain of the Trenton State prison at the time, and the sergeant in charge of her unit, had once worked under him and highly respected him. That really helped her a lot, in many ways. He knew the superintendent, Christine Mathison also. If Ali had any problems, she could call her cousin, who would investigate. But she rarely had any problems and never had to pull strings to clear them up. She was what would be considered the model inmate. Only a few times in her years there, did Ali have a problem.

SHE ONCE NOTICED THAT THERE was a mouse in her cell. She could hear it at night making chewing sounds. She went into the kitchen and secretly borrowed a non-toxic sticky pad mousetrap to put on the floor in her room. The next morning, she had caught a little, brown field mouse. She gently peeled it off the sticky pad with a pencil and dropped it into an empty red plastic margarine bowl, poking holes in the lid so it could breath. She was so excited that she found a pet. She fed it a cracker and showed it to the other girls on her wing. For some reason, a few of the black girls were literally horrified of the cute little thing and ran to the officer in charge to complain about her having a mouse. "EEK! A MOUSE! Oh my God!" You've got to be kidding me! She thought

Soon after, an officer went to her room and demanded, "Where is it?" "Where's what?" she replied. "You know exactly what I'm talking about!" "No I don't!" "Where's the mouse Durant?" "Oh that." "I should give you a charge for harboring a pet!" the officer yelled. "You've got to be kidding me! I was going to let it out at yard, but haven't gotten the chance to yet. I just caught it this morning. It's not my fault your prison has rodents." Ali replied.

So the officer took the mouse to the door, leading to the yard, and set it free while Durant watched. That's all she wanted, anyway. The little field mouse stunk so bad that she couldn't wait to get rid of it.

She didn't let the other inmates know that though, she wanted them to think that she was going to keep it as a pet. She was always getting threatened by some of the officers in her unit. Mostly for stupid little things like standing in front of someone else's room. It was considered loitering and you could be written up for it. She never argued back when they went off on her. She just figured that they had their own problems and needed to vent on someone. The inmates always got yelled at for hanging out in the laundry room just talking. It was a place that the officers couldn't supervise very well.

When they came in threatening the girls, she usually just stood there staring expressionlessly at them, or would just walk back to her cell without saying a word. It was a strange world to be in, and she had to be patient without reacting. You needed patience to stay sane in that environment.

Sometimes, if you needed to be transported to court or to the doctors, you had to wait hours in an empty holding cell before being seen. So you count blocks, pick the lint off your clothes, chew your nails or just think to yourself, rewinding past history in your mind or fantasizing about future events you might dream of happening. Always in shackles and handcuffs and strip-searched. She at times felt sorry for the female officers who had to strip search the big, fat, out of shape, nasty women who offended any one with their ugly nakedness. But who knows, just because she didn't like fat, doesn't mean others around her minded. I'm sure they were used to it.

Ali secretly enjoyed being in bondage. Every time she would get shacked and handcuffed, a part of her would get turned on. Then, to be escorted by someone in a uniform, with a gun on they're hip, it was really an exciting experience that she would never get tired of.

She could do without the strip-searching though. She thought that was way too invasive. She actually hated it and never got used to it, no matter how long she had been there. But you have to take the good with the bad. She thought

Ali would wait for signs from God to let her know when it was time for change. You couldn't avoid change no matter how used to something you got. Change was inevitable, especially there. But sometimes it was so slow that it was hardly noticed and sometimes it would come fast in waves.

ONE NIGHT, WHILE ALI WAS lying on her bed reading her bible, a thought came into her mind. There had to be a sacrifice of a ram before she could get out of prison. She later claimed that a spirit had told her this. She thought to herself, there are no rams around here anywhere. The spirit said it wasn't literal. It was a ram from the zodiac signs. Oh! She thought. So who did she know was a Capricorn? Joey!

The next day she called Joey to tell him that he was going to die, so she could be let out of jail. He laughed at her and said "What? Your going to kill me now?" she replied "Not me, them!" Then she went around telling everyone on her wing that Joey was going to be sacrificed by the spirits, so that she could be let out of prison.

Two weeks later...

All the women inmates in Z cottage, where called into the dayroom by the Lieutenants and Sergeants in charge. They said to the inmates, "We have some bad news, Katrina Hopkins died last night." She was an inmate three cells down from Durant.

Everyone was shocked! Then Ali yells out..."Does anyone know Katrina's Birthday?" One of the inmates yelled back "Yeah, March 29th, she was an Aries." "Oh shit!" Ali said out loud "I thought Capricorn was the ram, but that's right, it's not, it's the Goat; Aries is the ram."

Everyone who liked Katrina now wanted to kill Ali. They thought she was a witch who had actually cast a spell on her to get out of prison. So, a few of Katrina's friends were planning on setting Ali up to take her date from her when she got her parole date, soon after.

After four years of being in the same room, in the same building, Ali had to be moved for her own safety to Eastern Hall, another maximum security building, just because she said that stupid shit. Coincidence?

ANOTHER NIGHT, BEFORE THAT HAPPENED, while she lay sleeping, she was awakened by the sound of something popping outside her window. She saw shadows flickering around her room and looked out her window to see what it was.

There were about fifty balloons that were attached to ribbons wrapped around the razor wire right in front of her room. The wind was blowing the balloons against the wire, causing them to break. She thought to herself..."What does this mean?" Then the spirit said, "God sent you balloons to let you know that you have passed the test and can go home now." Ali didn't trust her inner voice, and still didn't believe it, but a couple weeks later, she was called to the office. They let her know that she was going before the parole board.

YET ANOTHER NIGHT, WHILE SHE lie sleeping, the sound of the officer walking down the hall, checking the doors to see if they were locked, woke her. A voice said to her at that time, "Ali, like Daniel in the lions den, those doors will open when God wants them to. If you don't believe me, get up right now and go push the door open." It was around three in the morning and Ali thought she was hallucinating, but decided to check it out anyway. So she got out of bed, walked to her door and pushed on it. The door swung open and slammed against the wall making a loud noise. The officer, who was heading back to her station, got startled from the noise and turned around to see what it was. Ali knew better than to leave her room; they could get her for attempting to escape or something. She just stood at her door waiting for the officer to come back and lock her in again.

When the woman got to her cell, she said, "Durant, you better quit that voodoo!" and closed the door and locked it up again. Ali just returned to her bed and went back to sleep.

Chapter 25

It seemed like every six months or so, she would hear from Joey the used car dealer. Whenever he and Star would break up, she would get a card from him letting her know that he missed her.

He would give her a phone number to call so she could call him. But conversation was boring to her. He never had anything important or significant to share with her. And he would always say stupid, idiotic things to her like "Hey, did anyone ever tell you you've got a nice ass?" He just sounded like a stupid Italian Guido to her. She had more important things to do than to listen to that dumb shit! She thought to herself.

After about a week or two of listening to him talk about her "Nice ass", she would try calling him and there would be a block on his phone. That meant he had gotten back together with his girlfriend.

But during the time he was alone, he would send her clothing packages or toiletries like shampoo, deodorant, soap and toothpaste with a toothbrush. She could have bought all that stuff on commissary, but he shipped her different products that the prison store didn't carry. He would also visit her and bring food packages, like bagels and fresh eggs. It was worth it to her to put up with his behavior. But she knew it wasn't going to last long.

Then, one day, about a year or two before Ali was released, Joey went to the prison to visit her and, out of the blue, he asked her to marry him.

She had said yes, but not because she was in love with him. She figured that no one else would want her when she got out, and he had been there for her when no one else was, she kind of felt that she owed him. She also knew he was a womanizer who could never stay faithful to any one woman no matter who they were. Deep down inside her, she felt it wasn't her destiny to marry someone like him no matter what she said.

He loved his women to wear short, sexy, tight dresses, high heels and lipstick at all times. She used to be like that, but she got used to being in sweat clothes with no makeup on and was just not into the whole image thing any longer. She was really into religion now, much more than she had been before she went away, and Joey hated it.

She was an artist and he never even paid attention to any other aspects of her being other than her big boobs and her "Nice ass." She thought he was very shallow. She felt that he was just trying to fulfill some lonely fantasy he was having, with the whole marriage thing.

He only thought he loved her at the moment, and those moments were as fleeting as his visits over the years.

About three months after Joey asked her to marry him, Ali introduced him to Holly who she desperately wanted to believe was her "friend."

Three days later, they were sleeping with each other. Go figure!

It was one of those emotional waves she had to ride out. It wasn't that she was hurt because he cheated on her either, she could care less about that. It was that she knew the world was never going to change, and that she had to go back out there again, someday soon.

After only six weeks with her so-called fiancé, banging her so-called friend, Joey had the nerve to show up at the prison begging Ali's forgiveness, telling her that he didn't love Holly; he loved her! Whatever!

Ali thought that Joey was an asshole, just doing the ole mental masturbation thing, since she was still in jail and no one was going to touch her anyway. Then Holly showed up at the prison, to visit Ali a few days after Joey's visit, literally crying her eyes out, "I love your man!" Ali asked her if she was Manic Depressive. I mean, how is someone stupid enough to allow herself to fall in love with a known womanizer and her supposed fiancé? Holly deserved what she got. Oh well! "And stop calling him my man!" she told her. "No one is my man. You made sure of that!"

Holly would visit Ali periodically through the years and tell her about the relationship she was having with Franc. How she was making love with him in the bed that Ali had bought for him. She would rub it in Ali's face how she would ride bikes with him through the countryside and spend endless hours with him alone. And Holly always made sure that Ali knew that she was on their minds the entire time. Sure! Eventually Holly and Franc got bored with each other again and they went their separate ways.

Did I mention that Holly was bi-sexual and that the only live in relationship she ever had was with another woman for six years before she met Franc? I can understand gay people because that's their preference, but I will never understand bisexuals. I believe that those kinds of people are the most deceiving of all people. They pretend to be having a "normal life" by marrying the opposite sex or dating them. But then one day their spouse and/or their children find out about their secret homosexual life. That's just wrong! Finding out about that kind of deception must hurt a person probably worse than any other heartbreak.

Joey continued to sleep with Ali's so-called friend up until her release from prison on February 19th, 1998. He had told her once before she got out that his relationship with Holly had been nothing and that is was over.

And the drama continued!

Chapter 26

After spending exactly five years and two weeks in her mental institution, prison or artist sanctuary, whatever it was, cleansing her mind of all the sin and negative energies that had put her there. In other words, trying to forget all the fucked up things that had happened to her, Ali had no other place to go when she got out, and had to be paroled to none other than Joey's house on the Manasquan River in Brandon, New Jersey.

She did however; desperately check out her other options before committing herself to that fate. But a halfway house in the bad section of Newark was just not that appealing to her then. So she would take her chances with the mini-mobster wannabe.

She couldn't be released without a place to go. Her entire family was now living in Orlando, Florida and even if she wanted to go there, it would have taken an additional six months for the transfer. Ali couldn't stand her family and would rather have been shot to death than to go live with them again. Her sister Jessica not one time bothered to visit her the entire time she was incarcerated and it was her friend Fenton who had caused Ali to wind up there.

All of Ali's closest friends had cats and she was highly allergic to them. She wouldn't have lasted three hours in a home with them, before dying of an asthma attack.

So it was either Joey's or staying in prison. Prison was really looking great again, but they wouldn't keep her without a reason, and she wasn't about to give them one.

On the day she got released, Joey was there to pick her up. He claimed he had waited five whole years for her. Some wait!

Ali had gotten the flu only three days before her release after all those years of staying healthy. She couldn't even get herself any Tylenol because she had been moved to Eastern Hall a few months before; which meant going outside in the freezing cold and standing in a medication line for forty-five minutes to get some.

She was extremely weak and lethargic by the time she had gotten into his car. Her fever was a burning 103 degrees. The first place they drove to was a nearby pharmacy so that Joey could get her some flu medication.

While Ali was sitting in his car in the pharmacy parking lot, Joey pulled out of his pocket an eight thousand dollar, marquee cut diamond engagement ring and asked her to marry him again. He put the ring on her finger after she swallowed her medication. She apprehensively said yes again.

It was a long drive back to Brandon from Clinton and she was very tired and weak from the virus. All she wanted to do was lie down. When she got into his house, she found a big "Welcome Home" sign and some balloons hanging in the living room. She thought, "How sweet and how typical, for him to try to over do it. Since he hadn't been faithful to his ex-convict fiancé.

But when she looked around the kitchen and living room, it didn't look like anyone had cleaned his house in years. There was at least and inch of ground in dirt on the kitchen linoleum floor. He reminded her that he had been seeing Holly and complained that she wouldn't even help him clean his house, while she was there fucking him. Within an hour of Ali being there, Joey wondered why she wasn't getting off the couch to help him clean up the mess.

Joey had thought he had been delivered a mail order bride, one who was only there for his carnal pleasures and personal needs. He had no compassion or any understanding of what it was like for her or any person, who had just spent the last five years in a small room, to be out in the world again.

Ali was so extremely vulnerable at that time and very sick with fever, but Joey still got angry and began yelling for her to get up and clean his house. Then he thought if he fed her, she'd be miraculously cured. So he took her out for some Japanese food. Ali loved Sushi and Miso soup, but she was still sick after she ate and just wanted to get so rest.

Joey had really changed in the five years she was away. He had an explosive personality, was easily angered and very abusive. She was not at all prepared for his bullshit. And then he told her that he was a coke addict. Not the caramel colored soda either. He said that Star had gotten him addicted while they were together. "That's just great!" she thought.

Three days after Ali got out of prison, Joey drove her to his dealership and as soon as they pulled into the lot, Ali noticed her so called friend Holly sitting at his desk with her feet up on the table as if she owned the place.

Ali called her outside to speak with her alone in her car. She was extremely pissed off at her for betraying her, but not for screwing Joey while she was away. She grabbed her ex-friend by her throat and began choking her, but then thought to herself, "This bitch is not worth it."

For the entire time Ali was in jail creating art, she had been sending it all to Holly to keep for her, but her so-called friend, sold most of her art behind Ali's back, then claimed to have given the money to Joey to help him out with his business. Ali had never given her permission to do that. And who to hell was she to think that she was still privy to Ali's once again fiancé? Ali got out of the car and began kicking the door and cursing at her as the back stabbing bitch drove off. Ali really just wanted to fuck her up for all the days that Holly spent with Franc while she had to sit back and watch it happen and couldn't do anything about it.

Adam Sr. had just showed up there to visit at the very moment Ali was kicking Holly's car. He and Joey began yelling at her to stop or she was going to go back to jail.

Within an hour, Joey was literally ripping the engagement

ring from her finger and threatening to throw her out of his house to cause a parole violation.

If she didn't have a place to stay, she would be in violation and sent back to prison. For the next three weeks that Ali was at his house, she was at his mercy, and what he did to her then was so wrong that she would never forget it.

After only a short time of being out of jail, still with a high fever, when Joey wasn't home, Ali walked out of his house, into his back yard and headed to the Manasquan River.

Then, in the bitter cold, she began to walk out into the freezing water. When she got waist high into the dark salty river, she thought to herself "If I plunge myself into the cold water, I'll die from hypothermia. I have to get out of this situation and I see no other way but death." And just when she was about to do it, a voice inside of her said, "Ali, have faith, you've come this far. He who endures to the end, the same shall be saved. To the end, Ali!" But when was the end? God damn it!

She turned around and went back inside to deal with it. She was both physically and sexually abused by him, had two of her ribs fractured. He choked her, picked her up one night and physically tossed her out of his house, throwing her down his steps so hard that the cross she had been given by her true love literally broke in half. Joey accused her of being a whore and verbally abused her to no end until she finally found someone to rescue her.

Ali realized that Joey must have been one of the guys who helped kill Rylan back in 1872. That's why Franc had feared seeing him in this life. Holly who had been Rebecca must have been in love with her own cousin back then and that's why she was so in love with Joey now. He was once her cousin. It was Holly's karmic punishment to know that Joey was really in love with Ali and that she would never truly have his heart. And would you believe that Holly actually had a younger brother in this life who, committed suicide by shooting himself in the head *while in a red barn*? Coincidence? No fucking way! What a screwed up situation! It was like some endless, bizarre, soap opera nightmare.

The first time Ali had gone into a grocery store after her incarceration for five years, she was blown away. It had been the A&P and when she got into the produce section her mind got sensory overload. It was like being on another planet or going from black and white to Technicolor. The extremely large room and the vibrant colors of the fruits and vegetables were overwhelming. The yellow peppers, red strawberries, bananas, oranges, purple plums, green peppers, carrots, lemons and limes were the most beautiful things she had ever seen and God created all of them.

How we take all these things for granted she thought. Imagine never seeing the moon again or smelling the scent of a candle or running barefoot on a beach feeling the sand between your toes. No one knows what it's like to not have those little things in their life until they've been locked away or have some serious handicap. Life is so fragile that we really shouldn't take any of it for granted. I guess you're really lucky if you can.

And then Ali was finally rescued…

Chapter 27

His name was also Joey, but Ali hated that name by then, so she called him Joseph. He had been running the Narcotics Anonymous meetings that she was ordered to go to.

Ali was on ISSP for the first year of parole (Intense Supervised Surveillance Program), because parole wanted her to attend a second program, for whatever reason, so they picked NA.

Ali never had a drug problem! Her problem was always the men and *their* addiction problems, but she figured that God had His reason for her to be there, or otherwise, it was a complete waste of her time. At least she could learn about addiction. She may not have been a drug addict searching for another high, but she was a love addict always searching for that ultimate take my breath away feeling that you usually got from a first kiss or when you fell in love with someone. She had learned to control her desires for the opposite sex, but it took years of heartache and abuse.

It turns out...

Ali eventually felt that she was in those meetings so the white knight could save her from the dark knight. Joseph was her angel, who came in his masculine white Mitsubishi to sweep her off her feet and drive her off into the sunset. Then four months later, she married him.

But it was only after Ali had gone to see Franc hoping to continue her delusions of a life with her soul twin. Unfortunately, Franc had some pit bull girlfriend of his come charging out to the driveway to confront her, while he hid himself inside the security and comforts of his home. The woman yelled for Ali to go away, that he didn't want to see her again. Ali was hoping that the woman would attempt to physically assault her so she could finally vent her anger onto someone and beat their ass. But the woman stood her distance, and only barked at her like some cowardly little dog.

It appeared that Franc didn't want to associate himself any longer with a known felon. Ali was too beneath him now. His parents even hated her for stabbing their son back in the day, as if he had absolutely nothing to do with it. Whatever! He wasn't her destiny! That was quite obvious. But Ali never again saw in her crystal ball the man that resembled him. That chapter was finally over and a new one began.

Ali believes that Franc's soul was also the reincarnation of Richard Lovelace who lived in the 1600's and was a cavalier poet. Franc certainly looked a lot like him. She thought that perhaps her visions of him in uniform came from that particular lifetime. Lovelace had been incarcerated in that life and died fairly young of poverty. He had written two poems that would eventually become his legacy. One of them was to "Lucasta" Going to the Wars where he spoke of honor. The other was to "Althea from prison. Stone walls do not a prison make nor iron bars a cage." Could those poems have been about the souls of Elizabeth and Rebecca competing for his love even as far back as that lifetime? Did he love Lucy or was it Althea? And which one was Ali? It seems that Lovelace was madly in love with Lucy (Lucasta) not Althea. But as soon as Lucy heard he was gone, she married another. Perhaps Ali wasn't either of them. Who knows, but she really loves his poetry.

The irony is, that while Ali was in jail, on occasion she would get a package addressed to Althea. Someone would misspell her name. She began to think that Althea was once misspelled.

Ali also believes that Richard Lovelace had been bi-sexual and that Franc had carried some of those traits with him into this lifetime. She always had her suspicions of his preferred sexuality. Then again, Ali always thought that most men were

Bi. She would often joke and say, "How can a woman compete with a man? You can't compete with masculine muscles and a big rod to put up your butt. Perhaps she suffered ever so slightly from penis envy. It drove her mad to think that she didn't stand a chance with some of the most handsome men in Hollywood because they preferred being with another man and not with a woman. As if she was ever going to be out in Hollywood again dating any movie stars. How sad it is for women! She once said to me.

For some reason Franc was the only person Ali ever met, whom she believed she had known from a previous life and had been reincarnated. She never again found another person who she claimed she knew from another lifetime.

A few years after Ali was released from prison, Franc's mother passed away. The trauma was so great for him that he wound up in a mental institution from a breakdown. That's when he turned to God again for comfort. He began writing spiritual hymns just like he did when he was Martin Luther. If it's meant to be, perhaps one day his hymns will be heard by everyone and he will get what he always wanted in this life, to be famous again.

AFTER ALI MARRIED JOSEPH,

Joey, who had spent five years fantasizing about her, was now realizing he had screwed up. He even cried to her, begging her for forgiveness, wanting her to go back home with him, but Ali wasn't stupid. She knew he was an abuser just like her first husband and a womanizer like her daughter's father and there was no way in hell she would ever put herself at the mercy of someone like that ever again. She would rather die!

They stayed friends however over the years, and he eventually bought himself a big country style restaurant in upstate New York. He even let Ali name it for him. Joey had his problems just like the rest of us, but one day on a cold October morning, he boarded up his restaurant to do some time in prison for tax evasion.

He continued to spend occasional weekends with Holly

until then. Holly never had any children and still sleeps around with a few of Ali's friends here and there. For some reason that still seems to bother her after all these years.

ALI NEVER HAD HER FATHER give her away at her second wedding either. No one she knew came to that wedding. Her family said they were not going to waste money traveling from Florida for a marriage that wasn't going to last. No one Joseph knew went to it either because he had kept the marriage a secret from his entire family and all his friends until afterwards.

Ali had found a beautiful white wedding dress at a consignment shop near her apartment with a matching Vail for a hundred and twenty-five dollars.

They got married on the beach in Cape May, New Jersey by the mayor himself on June 13, 1998. St. Anthony's day to the Catholics and Joseph was Catholic.

Ali's Wedding

It was so romantic! They took a horse and buggy ride around town after the ceremony. Hundreds of people were at their wedding, but not one person they knew, only tourists and beach goers.

They slept at a bed and breakfast called Poor Richards Inn.

Ali had gotten St. Anthony tattooed on her lower back. St. Anthony was the finder of lost things, and she felt as though she was once lost and now found. Unfortunately, by the time she was found, she had a gamut of psychological problems far worse then ever before.

She wanted to strip in the clubs again and went back to a bar in Bound Brook, where she danced before she went away. The owner was glad to have her back, but the industry had changed in five years. They now had lap dancing, which they didn't have before. And that meant being really close to the customers in a really private area, alone with them.

Joseph would drive her to work and pick her up afterwards. He was so thrilled when he saw all the money she was making. It was most likely because he was thinking that she would be able to take care of his financial needs and wants. Or who knows, maybe he was happy that he could go on with his own life without having to worry about hers any longer.

Ali kept dancing a secret from her parole officer because it was a violation to be working in a bar.

She had remembered what a gypsy woman once told her. The woman said that Ali would be married three times in this life and her second marriage would only last two years.

It wasn't long before Ali became very angry at or resentful of Joseph. Even though he had rescued her and rented her, an apartment with the little savings he had, he stayed living at his mother's house after they were married. He would spend long weekends with his daughter and wouldn't invite Ali along. It was as if she was his mistress and not his wife.

He wouldn't even wear his wedding ring. She felt hopelessly alone. At least in prison there was always someone to talk to. Ali wasn't used to being completely alone in some strange apartment without anyone to keep her company.

There were so many things about him that bothered her, but the most significant thing was that she really wasn't in love with him. She had been so betrayed by so many men in her life that it was impossible for her to let herself go and really fall in love with anyone any longer. Her heart was completely jaded! She didn't believe a word he told her. With no trust, there's nothing but resentment.

Ali had finally fulfilled her fantasy of a white wedding that she had had for the five years she spent behind bars; but that's all it was: just a fantasy.

Her father hadn't even given her away and he died a few years later.

The reality was that she didn't want to be in another prison and being married to him, in her mind, was just another form of imprisonment.

The truth was, Joseph had gotten her pregnant and DYFS informed her that as soon as she had the child, they would take it away from her at the hospital. Her husband didn't help matters when he told her that he didn't want another child anyway. She took it that he didn't want a child with her.

Either way, he went with her to get an abortion. That was most likely the thing that pushed her over the edge to run from the pretend marriage.

She also had to register now as a felony sex offender under the Megan's Law, which was passed right before her release. She had to register with the police once a year for the next fifteen years or whenever she moved as a Tier one offender. Tier three being the worst. So even though she was married, she couldn't have a child until she was off parole in five years.

The charges she had been found guilty of in the beginning had been reduced to "First degree and second degree liability for the conduct of another." They began as Accomplice Charges, but on appeal, got reduced to liability.

She was no accomplice, but they held the twenty-five year old mother liable for the conduct of Fenton Noor, a sixty-year old man, because she was stupid enough to trust him with her children.

BACK WHEN IT ALL BEGAN in 1991

There was a mass hysteria going on in the country at that time of child sexual abuse cases. Most of which the cases eventually got dropped or overturned for many of the accused. It finally came out in the media that the child psychologists and even the prosecutors were coaching the children as to what to say while in court.

Even though Ali didn't have the huge amounts of money that it would have taken to fight her case, the appellate division eventually got her sentence reduced to "the liability of the conduct of another." There really was no proof that she had deliberately sold her child to the predator, but they felt that she should have known better than to let a man babysit her daughter. Ali was only doing what all those other women did. She was following the advise of her sister and got screwed because she was a disrespected stripper. So whatever happened to Jessica and the other women who allowed their daughters to be in the care of this man? I'll tell you what happened to them, nothing! Not a damn thing happened to any of the other women and I am quite sure that Fenton's daughter knew exactly what he was doing with those kids because she had been molested herself by him.

One of the parole panel persons had told her "You're too trusting" when she went up for parole. He also said "You poor kid! The reason I'm calling you a kid is because you look like one." She *had* been too trusting!

Not any longer! She would never trust another guy for as long as she lived. For that matter, she would even find it hard to trust ever trust women.

Ali was so hurt and so lonely. She missed her children and really wanted another one badly, but she knew that even if she were the best mother in the world this time, she would still have it taken away from her. Her resentment towards the world became even greater than ever before.

She began doing all the things that she had been accused of doing years before when they took her children away and threw her in jail. She began slipping her hands into the guy's pants, pleasuring them while doing lap dances. She smirked out of anger while doing it. Or she would tell the customers interested in her that she would meet them in a hotel room afterwards, take their money and slip out the back before they would notice she was gone. But the owner of the club she was working in found out about it and called her to tell her that the police were searching for her to arrest her for prostitution.

He warned her not to go back there because he liked her. She got scared! She was afraid she would be arrested for a parole violation, if nothing else. So she stopped dancing.

She enrolled into a massage school and began studying massage. After a few months, she went out and found herself some clients. She was making two hundred dollars an hour going to people's homes to massage them.

Then one day, she found her husband driving a woman in his car that he claimed he had taken out to lunch. But Ali sensed that he had been cheating on her and told him that for every woman he could have sex with, she would do ten guys and get paid for it. Then shortly after that, she secretly joined an escort service, and told him that she was just being a masseuse.

Ironically, one day, she got a call from the agency to go to Arnold's house in Rumson. He used to be her boyfriend and they thought it would be a cute surprise for her to show up as his escort. He was surprised, all right. He couldn't believe that his beautiful, sexy Ali had resorted to escorting and she couldn't believe that her famous rock star ex-fiance, who could get anyone he wanted at one point, had to be reduced to paying for an escort. They talked for hours and he told her what had happened to him, why he had been let go by the band. But she had already guessed what had happened because she knew him. He told her that her premonition had come true and that he had been in a bad car accident and had to have his hip replaced. She was surprised to hear that since a part of her never really believed she had the ability to foresee anything.

It's so funny how things turn out. They had both been so successful at one time in their own ways, but fate would take a turn for the worst for both of them. He wound up auctioning off everything in his mansion and eventually moving south. She wound up leaving her husband three days before their first year anniversary and moving to Paterson, eighty miles north, just to get away from it all. She wanted to start a new life somewhere where no one would know her past. And that's when she found me, Randy A. DeOrio.

Chapter 28

Ali told me that she wanted to establish base, so together, we moved into a beautiful, red brick house that overlooked the entire valley of Paterson. Our landlord was an old Ukrainian man who was living with his girlfriend of fourteen years, but refused to marry her. They thought we were the perfect couple. Ali was suffering from an adjustment disorder, along with every other disorder, and was scared to be alone in a strange city, so she stayed with me 24/7 for the first two years that we were together.

I took her to get her parole transferred and to meet her new parole officer. She couldn't get a regular job, because no one would hire a felony sex offender while still on parole. So I let her help me calibrate police cars all over the state. I had been doing that since I was fourteen years old. She hated the police, mostly because she feared them. But after hanging out with me for two years and meeting nothing but police officers whom had treated her like a person and not like a criminal she eventually got past her fears. Well, she stopped panicking at the sight of them anyway.

She even made a few friends of high rank in Paterson. She had dinner with the mayor, became very good friends with the deputy major, who just recently passed away, and even painted a huge painting that she donated to the Sheriff's department. The Governor was even there at the unveiling. It's now hanging in the Passaic County Jail. How ironic!

JUST WHEN SHE WAS BEGINNING to heal again from the trauma that had found her, I left her alone one night in March of 2001 so I could work. I got home very late and she was already asleep, but not on the bed in her bedroom. She was sleeping on the sofa in the living room, where I usually slept. I didn't think much about it and went to sleep in her comfortable bed. I was awakened at 9AM when she began shaking me. She started rambling about a dream she had the night before.

She said her parole officer Thomas Gouthe, had come into the house and raped her. I said "You woke me up to tell me about a dream? Are you kidding me?" I got upset because I was really tired and to be awakened for something as stupid as a dream was ridiculous. Then she asked me "What would you do if it was real?" It was then, that I began to get suspicious and asked "What? Was Gouthe here last night?" She said, "Yes."

That's when I sat up and demanded that she tell me everything that happened. So she did.

She said that around 10 PM the night before, the doorbell rang. She went to the door to find her parole officer standing there. It was very unusual that he would come so late and she began to panic, thinking he was there to violate her for something. She had gone to a strip club in Paterson only a week before to audition, and thought that he had found out about it. She wasn't allowed to be in a place that served alcohol while on parole.

Then she noticed he was wearing his bulletproof vest. She asked him why. He told her he had been going to other parolee's homes that night in areas of Paterson that weren't very safe.

He was wearing his badge around his neck, as usual, and had handcuffs on his belt and of course, he was carrying a gun in his holster. It was very intimidating to the petite blonde woman on parole. All alone, late at night, with just him and her in her house, she had to let him enter inside. What was she going to say, "No, you can't come in, you scare me!"

When he got inside, he asked her what she'd been doing lately. She really thought he knew, and if she didn't admit it to him, he would get angry and violate her, so she told him how she had gone to the "Hitching Post" to audition, but she never went back there to work, even though they gave her a date to.

Then, he just casually sat down on her wooden rocking chair in her living room and asked her to demonstrate her performance. She questioned, "You want me to dance for you?" He said "of course, why not?" "Ok" she replied. So she began moving her hips as if slow dancing. The fear was still in the back of her mind that he would violate her if she didn't comply or even if she did.

Wearing long baggy brown pants and a long sleeved brown striped shirt that didn't appear to be seductive at all, she wondered why he was doing this. Then he asked her to take her clothes off and let her hair down. She always kept her hair up in a bun. She did what he asked and stripped down to total nakedness.

Then he grabbed her by her wrist, pulling her over to him so he could kiss her. He stood up and pushed her face forward against the armoire putting her hands up against it, he stood behind her naked body, pulled her hair aside and whispered into her left ear. "You're a bad girl!" Then he began smacking her ass so hard that he busted the blood vessels, leaving severe bruising all over her rear end.

While he was doing that to her, he had managed to unbutton his pants that were now dropped to his ankles. He turned her around and pushed her down to face his erection and held her head in his hands motioning for her to suck what appeared to her to be a very, very, disappointingly small penis. She thought to herself, "Can someone really have sex with something this small? How to hell did he manage to have a child? And why is he doing this to me? If someone is going to rape me, why would he bring this to the crime scene?" For a brief moment, she had fantasized that he was going to pick her up and carry her into the bedroom to make mad passionate love to her, with something that would actually bring her to climax. He wasn't bad looking and dressed very nicely at the office. But he only wanted a selfish blowjob with his lack of manhood. I guess that's why he carried a gun, she thought. He had to over compensate for his lack of masculinity elsewhere. "The nerve to be raping me with this!" she thought to herself. "And why did he have to hit me so damn hard? I wasn't that bad!"

She pulled him out of her mouth just before he ejaculated, allowing his disgusting man goo to shoot all over her breasts. She didn't want to have to clean his body fluids off of her fairly new carpeting, and she most definitely was not going to allow him to do that in her mouth. Even thought she spit, and was not a swallower, she didn't want anyone to do that to her any more, either way.

After he finished relieving himself, she looked up at him while still on her knees and asked, "Are we done yet?"

He calmly said, "Yes." "Can I get dressed now?" she continued. "Sure go ahead." he replied. So she got up off her knees, but before she put her clothes back on, she went to the linen closet in the hallway, got out a white washcloth and continued to the bathroom to wash her self off.

When she finished, she tossed the rag on the floor back in the hallway and went to the living room again, where her clothes were, so she could get dressed.

He was dressed and ready to leave. He walked to her front door and said, "See you next month." Her visits to the parole office were only once a month, and she had just had her visit the week before. Then he left.

As he was walking to his car, she yelled out to him "Good-bye!" but he didn't turn around, he didn't say good-bye back to her. There was no response. She thought he might not have heard her. So she yelled again, this time louder, "Good-bye!" He just kept walking and didn't turn around. He got into his car and drove away as if she didn't even exist. As if nothing had just transpired between the two of them.

Ali didn't know what to think. She couldn't believe what had just happened. In her mind, he was going to go back to his office the following day and brag to his co-workers how he had just gotten a free blowjob from that wacky blonde bimbo he had as a client.

She felt so humiliated, but it wasn't the first time someone had forced himself on her. She just had to accept it and be thankful that he really didn't hurt her or put the cuffs on her to send her back to jail for whatever story he would make up to his supervisors.

She laid on the sofa in the dark, fully dressed, wondering why this had just happened to her. What the fuck is wrong with the people on this planet? She thought to herself as she closed her eyes and fell asleep.

Chapter 29

~~~~~~

After she told me this story,
I jumped out of bed to get dressed, and told her that we were going downtown to the police station right now to press charges on him. I was extremely protective of her and couldn't believe Gouthe had the balls to come into my house and rape my friend. It's a territorial guy thing! I really wanted to beat **HIS** senseless ass! She began to panic with fear and cry, insisting that we do absolutely nothing about it. She feared retaliation from the parole people. She said there was no way they were going to tell anyone what had just happened.

I responded with, "Listen, I have a few detective friends down at the police station. Why don't we just go talk to one of them? I calmed her down and she hesitantly went with me to the Paterson PD. I took the washcloth with us, even though she said she had washed it and thought there was no more DNA evidence on it any longer.

It just so happened that there was a female detective working there that day who handled the sexual assault cases. She reminded Ali of a corrections officer at the prison she had been in, the same one in fact, who had saved her pet mouse. Ali immediately took to her. Her name was Officer Bodanski and she handled Ali very professionally. She was such a nice person and was genuinely concerned with Ali's frame of mind. She had even pulled me aside and told me to really take care of her. I replied, "Of course I will! She's my family."

Ali was very paranoid about the whole police thing and thought they would all conspire against her, lose the rag to protect their fellow officer and then throw her back in jail for trying to get one of them into trouble.

The detective assured her that he was not a fellow police officer and that she didn't even know him. I suggested that we call an attorney to represent her before we continued. I knew of a good one who was Jewish and a great friend of mine. She seemed to trust Jewish people more than anyone else. His name was Miles Burnstein and he came to the police station as soon as he was called.

It's not that they didn't believe her. They just wanted to make sure she wasn't just trying to get her parole officer into trouble. After all, he was a twelve-year veteran who had a clean record. It didn't make any sense to them. Why would he do something like this now?

Miles kept asking her the same question. "Are you sure that you have Gouthe's semen on the cloth and not someone else's?" she said "Like who's? Tyron's from down the street in the projects?" Exactly! "I don't even know a Tyron or anyone else around here, because I haven't hung out with anyone besides Randy since I moved here." But she also warned them that she had washed the rag off, so there might not be anyone's semen on it.

They took her statement and eventually sent her home to wait for the DNA tests to come back. It took six weeks to find out if there was any evidence left on the rag that we had brought to the Police Station.

Ali had been very paranoid before this whole incident happened, but now, she was completely insane with fear. She kept the front door dead bolted even with me in the house and refused to leave under any circumstances. She didn't want me leaving her alone, but wouldn't come with me. She was horrified that the police were going to come get her, to take her back to jail, or that her parole officer would come back to the house to kill her.

We fought constantly until I convinced her to get some professional help. I took her to the Mental Health Clinic, in downtown Paterson and helped her get a psychologist to treat her. The psychiatrist there, wanted to put her on Anti-psychotic medication, but she refused to take ANY medication. Not even Valium to calm her nerves.

She was waking up in the middle of the night with full-blown anxiety attacks that drove me crazy. I felt so helpless because I didn't know how to assist her.

I would just talk to her and remind her that this was something that she had experienced before and was going to get through it again, like all the other times. She had to ride out the wave.

Eventually, she began collecting SSI for mental disability and that took some of the pressure off of me for having to support us both. I became her payee, that made me responsible for taking care of her, and life went on.

Six weeks after they had taken the specimen for DNA testing, the female detective called her to inform her that the DNA matched Gouthe's and that he had been arrested that very same morning.

He eventually pled guilty and received only three years probation. He ended his career in law enforcement and most likely lost his pension. Her attorney filed suit, but she only received a small amount of compensation for her ordeal. She did, however, receive an official written apology from him.

Big Deal! As if that was going to make her feel any better.

She asked me once, " Was it the size of his penis that meant the size of my victim compensation?" "No!" I told her. "It was because he sexually assaulted a person that society deemed as being of low moral standing." Whatever! He was warned never to go near her again and he never did!

To all the men out there who think that they can rape women or molest children, the moral of the story is: Even a small penis can get you into BIG trouble!

To all the women out there who think that they're with someone they can trust with their children, beware of hidden agendas!

Chapter 30

~~~~~~

She finished out her parole on February 9th of 2003. She had continued visits to the parole office once a month to report, but no one from parole ever came to her house again, after that incident, to check up on her.

She knew that her credibility in this life was non-existent from the first time she had ever walked into the prosecutor's office to tell her side of the story back in 1991. She knew that if there were ever any kind of situation that would happen, the courts would most likely take the other person's word over hers.

This means, having to really be careful not to put herself into any compromising situations for anyone to even question. Without her having concrete evidence to help her, she would be completely screwed. Hell, in her case, the courts would most likely throw out her evidence even if she had some.

She doesn't trust anyone for good reason, not even her closest friends. She thinks the worst when something happens, and thinks that something bad is going to happen when anything changes her daily routine, even in the slightest bit.

I was really getting a good education on how to handle women of abuse. She was a true victim who had overcome time and time again, the mental challenges that come with remembering the pain. She still tries to keep the faith, but it's not easy. Her psychologist said that the anxiety attacks are repressed emotions trying to surface. That makes complete sense! But it doesn't make them any less horrifying.

I had spent endless hours with her in emergency rooms

when she was having those anxiety and/or panic attacks, when she thought she was dying or someone else was.

I've lived with this person nearly eleven years and it's been a challenge to say the least.

The one thing that I have to admit is a real challenge when hanging out with her, is having to go with her, once a year, to the Paterson Police Station so she can register for the Megan's Law. No one ever looks at her as a sex offender; she's a beautiful woman. They always look at me and think I am. But because she's afraid to go into elevators alone, she won't go there unless I go with her.

We just recently went for her to register again, and I have to admit that the elevator there is one of the smallest, most rickety, old elevators I've ever been in, and we have to take it to the fourth floor. They won't even let us use the stairs.

It doesn't make any sense to me why she has to register for that law. She's not a pedophile and she wasn't even there when the crime was committed. The only crime she should have been guilty of, at best, might have been neglect, but she didn't leave her kids alone or with someone she knew was high on drugs, so I don't get it. They think she knew he was a pedophile, but I doubt it. Knowing her as well as I do, she was most likely going to have Fenton very hurt after she found out about her daughter. If they thought she wasn't paying attention, and didn't care if someone was abusing her child, that's neglect. I just don't get these laws sometimes! It's not right that she falls under it! It's just plain weird! Ali thinks that God is allowing all this to happen to remind her that there are some very disturbed people on this planet and that she better NEVER let her guard down again.

I do have to say, in spite of all her disorders, she is one of the most nurturing, kindest, most talented people that I've ever met and she has proven to me time and again, that no matter what challenges we face in this life, we can still overcome them and try to do our best to take care of ourselves while struggling to survive. She is a true survivor! She doesn't drink alcohol, and doesn't do drugs, she tries to take care of herself and she's always trying to become a better person. She even became a Nationally Certified Massage Therapist in 2007 because she wants to help others get relief from their anxieties.

Unfortunately, she's too paranoid to be alone in a room with anyone to actually give him or her a massage, so she doesn't practice that often.

River Rocks

Chapter 31

Even now, her older children are still a very sensitive subject to her. She tries not to think about them, because it really hurts what happened to her family, but she thanks God everyday that they are all alive and hopefully doing well.

She had no idea what was going on with her children while she was in jail, nor would it have mattered if she knew, because there was nothing she could do about it anyway. Her poor daughter was passed around from foster home to foster home until she was fifteen years old.

It wasn't until Ali was let out of prison that her daughter met a boy in her school who she began dating. He brought her home to meet his parents and they adored her. She wanted a family so badly that she talked them into adopting her. But before that could happen, she had to get Ali's permission, because she still had legal rights to her children. So, while Ali was living in Paterson, she got a surprise phone call from Amanda. Amanda explained the situation and asked her mother nicely to relinquish her parental rights so that she could be adopted. Ali told her she would do so if it would make her happy. So she met the attorneys downtown and signed her rights away.

For years, the state had been taking her back and forth to court, trying to make that happen. They had managed to get Amanda's father into court to get his signature, but Ali fought them tooth and nail, only to give in, when she felt Amanda was old enough to make her own choices and when Amanda asked her nicely, she couldn't refuse. She could never refuse her children anything when they asked for it nicely.

Amanda has a family now and, once in a while, will call Ali to say hi or tell her about something happening in her life, but for the most part, the two of them don't have a relationship.

They had met a few times over the years and Ali talked with her daughter about what had happened that fateful night back in 1991. Amanda told her, "She had been molested by Fenton, over a course of a few months." Ali asked her why she never said anything to anyone while it was happening, and Amanda said: "Fenton had threatened to kill my mother if I did." So Amanda was trying to protect her mother by not telling her of the abuse.

Ali asked her why she had said on the witness stand that, "Every time I told my mother", meaning she had told her more than once, " she would smack me in the face and send me to my room." Amanda said that she knew that didn't happen, but when Ali asked her to recant her statement to give her some peace, she refused.

Amanda still harbors so much repressed guilt, because she knows in her heart, that it was her testimony that helped get her mother convicted. Ali tried to comfort her and convince her that it wasn't her fault, that she was only a child and was manipulated by the authorities, but it still doesn't make her feel any less guilty.

Even though it wouldn't bring back all the years that she wasted behind bars and wouldn't bring back her little children that she lost, it would give Ali back some peace of mind to know that the truth has finally been told.

She may not have been the ideal mother, but she wasn't a mother who would allow someone to deliberately abuse her children. Amanda still won't give that to her. She won't even have a relationship with her brother Tyler who still calls his mother frequently asking her why his sister doesn't want anything to do with him. He doesn't understand, because he never did anything to hurt her.

Ali had to explain to him, on a few occasions, that Amanda has another family now and if she associates with this one, she feels that she would be betraying them. They have given her so much that she feels she at least owes them her loyalty.

TYLER WAS PLACED IN A home with a married couple, that also had a boy his age. But according to him, he was abused by them for years and forced to take Ritilin. He eventually ran away from their home, never to speak with them again, and is now living with a friend in Toms River, NJ.

Amanda had convinced him, when their mother went away, that she was a very evil person. He became very frightened of even the thought of her and never wanted to visit her while she was away. He even gave away a blanket she had crocheted for him, thinking it was demon possessed.

Ali found out where he was living when she got out of jail, and went to see him. As soon as he saw his mother, he broke down and cried. He knew that he had been lied to, all those years, to be frightened of her like he was. He told his mother that he never wanted to be out of her life again and to this day, they still speak with each other quite often. He had even moved in with her for a while a few years back, but then he met a girl online and moved out with her. He's now twenty-four years old. He adores his baby sister and every time he visits her, he brings her a gift. In spite of growing up without his mother, he has turned out to be a handsome, loving son who works hard and appreciates his blessings.

ADAM JR. LIVED WITH HIS grandmother until he was fourteen years old. It was right around the time when Ali got out of prison that Adam Sr. kidnapped Adam Jr. and took him to live in North Carolina.

Ali had only gotten to spend a few months with him when she got out.

Someone Ali knew had told her, that Adam Sr. had been seen at the methadone clinic in Asbury Park and that he was doing heroin. She couldn't believe that he was doing such a dangerous, addictive drug, so she asked him and he admitted it to her.

She was surprised and saddened too, because she knew the problems that came with doing opiates.

The last time Ali saw her son before he was taken to North Carolina, he had gone over to her apartment and asked her for fifty dollars. She told him that he could have anything he wanted from her, but she wanted the truth first. She asked him if the money was really for his father, so he could go cop some dope. As she had suspected, he admitted that it was. She never gave him the money and a few days later her son and his father disappeared.

She called the police to report the kidnapping, but nothing was ever done about it because of who she was or what she was. No one cared that a father had taken his fourteen-year old child from his convicted felon mother.

Five years later, when his grandmother passed away, Adam Sr. and Adam Jr. showed up at the funeral and she finally got to see her son again. He told her that his father had forced him to go away with him. Away from his friends and family and all that he knew, and had to live out in the middle of nowhere. He told her how he had to watch his father and his father's girlfriend sticking needles in their arms daily, for years, and how he went hungry and crazy from the boredom at times. Thank God his father never encouraged him to use the needle or that dangerously addictive drug. In spite of his addiction and his son's exposures to it, he was actually very protective of Adam Jr. and would not allow him to practice the same behavior.

His father would take him to work with him, and he taught his son the trade of building homes in construction. Adam Jr. is really a hard working carpenter now, just like his father. He is also a very angry young man, who feels that his mother abandoned him and he resents his father for the things he has put him through. He has good reason to feel the way he does.

She only managed to see him one time after the funeral. His baby sister was six months old. All of her children went to visit their sister at that time. It was a nice reunion for her. But after it was over, she didn't hear from her son again for years. As a matter of fact, it was his girlfriend who contacted Ali out of the blue a couple years later. She had left a message for Ali to call her, that she had bad news to tell her about her son. Ali immediately began panicking, thinking he had gotten killed in a car accident or something. She returned her call as soon as she had gotten the message. His girlfriend told her that Adam was in jail for assaulting someone and needed seventy-five hundred dollars to bail himself out.

She didn't have that kind of money and couldn't help him. But she drove to Waldwick and was able to see her grandson for the first and only time in his life. He was six months old. She took him out and bought him clothes and toys and spent nearly five hundred dollars on him that day. She also sent her son some books from the bookstore and put money in his commissary for him.

He called her a few times, while incarcerated, and spoke with her, but that was all. He was let out of the county jail a few months later and she has never heard from him again.

Tyler, who has established somewhat of a relationship with his brother, told his mother that he took his family and went back to North Carolina. She really has no idea what ever happened to him and doesn't even pry. She knows her children are living their lives.

They are all grown up now and if they choose to disown her, that's their choice.

Ali has her hands full these days with her six-year-old daughter. She spends all of her time trying to keep Sophia happy. She's at a summer camp now and in a few weeks will be heading off to first grade. Life is usually calm for the both of them, for the most part. But it hasn't always been that way and I'm sure another storm is yet to come soon. This is, most likely, only the calm before that storm.

Having Sophia was the best thing that ever happened to her, and yet, has been one of the most challenging of all the battles she's had to fight in her life. I'm sure it's a war that will continue though. She just takes life "one day at a time." as they say. Sometimes, that's all we can do, and pray for a positive outcome. Oh wait, I'm getting ahead of myself. Sophia hasn't come yet!

Chapter 32

It all began when Ali decided to go back to school. It was shortly after she had begun therapy with her psychologist, which was soon after the assault from her PO, back in 2002.

She enrolled into the Katherine Gibbs College for graphic design in Montclair, NJ. She loves photography and wanted to learn how to use the Photoshop program so she could fix her photos. But there was so much more to learn that she wanted a degree in that field.

She was faithfully going to every class and her GPA was at least a 3.85. She made the Deans list every semester and was doing very well. She had made a few friends and would hang out with them after class in the quaint, artsy, college town of Montclair.

All was well, except that she needed a few of the programs that cost at least a thousand dollars and she didn't have the money for them.

Our friend Eli, (a nice old Jewish man, she and I met at a Barnes & Nobles when she first moved here), worked for this huge marketing company, and he told her that he would talk to one of the guys in the art department who might be able to download some of the design programs onto her laptop so she wouldn't have to pay for them.

Eli said that this guy, Noah, owed him a big favor. When Noah had gotten his car stolen a few months before, Eli was driving him into work everyday and then, home again afterwards until he got himself another car.

Ali remembered Eli talking about him quite often and

making fun of him because he was so young and afraid to travel alone anywhere far. Eli would tell her that young people should be adventurous and not afraid to go anywhere. Ali reflected on his words and agreed, since she had taken six trips to Florida in one year alone when she was only twenty-three, by car no less, and wasn't the least bit afraid.

How dangerous that was, though. What if the car had broken down? She never thought of that, she just loved being spontaneous and going on long trips. The open road was nothing but pure freedom and it was always thrilling to fantasize about the destination. She always hated returning and the trip seemed that much longer on the way back. But she would put in a good CD and voila instant company!

ELI BROUGHT HER TO THE company building one day and introduced her to Noah, one of the graphic artists that worked there. She didn't think much of anything about him because she was just focused on her mission to borrow some expensive software programs from the company so she could do her college courses.

He was very nice to her and installed all the programs she needed, all the ones she had asked him for. He even gave her his cell phone number and told her if she had any problems with any of the programs that she could call him and he wouldn't mind. She thought that was very generous of him.

She wound up having to call him as soon as she got home that same day when she tried to use the programs. She was just learning Quark Express and had no clue how to use it and thought, since he's in the business, he must know a lot about the programs, so she just wanted to pick his brain for all the information.

He went over to her house to help her as soon as he had finished work. They sat on her bed most of the time with her laptop in front of them. He was dressed very casual, as Fridays were dress down day in that company and it was Friday. He was wearing a baseball cap on his head, and he kept his head down most of the time, so she didn't really see his face, but he seemed like the typical young Jewish guy to her.

After working in the strip clubs all those years, she had pretty much tuned guys out and didn't pay any attention to what anyone looked like anymore. I even made fun of her for that. I once introduced her to the same guy three days in a row and each time, she would ask me who he was. I don't know if it's her short-term memory problem or not, but it was pretty weird. I thought she was just kidding, but she wasn't.

She told me it was the guy's clothes, each day he wore a different outfit and he looked like a different person to her. She said she thought his face was unattractive so she didn't want to look at it, but I informed her of all the girlfriends this guy had. She laughed and replied "Quantity does not mean quality!"

I thought he was a nice-looking guy, but I'm a guy, what do I know about what women think is attractive.

Now back to Noah...

After he left her, they began talking on the phone. I mean for hours at a time. I asked her "What do you guys find to talk about for all those hours?" I've never seen anything like it before. I counted nine hours one night. That's crazy! I knew she was lonely and a yenta, but damn!

She said she was intrigued with his mind, that he was very smart and such a great conversationalist. She told me she had fallen in love with his mind! Imagine that!

She didn't even know what he looked like and he had been on her bed for hours. He must not have been that impressive to her. She said she had read his palm while he was there and saw a few women in his hand, but thought nothing of it.

About a week later, after at least forty hours on the phone together, she asked him if she could take him out to lunch. It was the least she could do, after helping her with her computer programs. He told her that he would have to ask Eli first since Eli was her boyfriend. She thought he was out of his mind and insisted that it was absolutely not true.

Apparently Eli had been telling his co-workers that Ali was

his young, beautiful, sexy girlfriend. She was actually flattered by it, and really didn't care what he told them. She didn't know any of them anyway and didn't care what any of them thought. She still doesn't!

Noah told Ali he had been pining over his boss, Christine, for the past five years. He admitted to her that he was madly in love with Christine. That's one of the things he talked about with her during their long conversations. He even gave her all the intimate details of their flirtatious playing together, but she was married and wasn't going to leave her husband, house and child for someone like him, not to mention she was his boss.

Whatever!

When Noah asked Eli if he would mind the two of them going out to lunch together, Eli told him that Ali was her own person and could do whatever she wanted.

So, Ali showed up at Noah's job one day to take him out to lunch. While she was waiting in her Jeep for him to come out, some really overweight, skanky- blonde with straggly hair and glasses came walking out of the building and went right over to her window, looked at her, gave her a nasty look, snubbed her nose and walked away. "Who the hell was that?" Ali thought. Then some old lady, who seemed like a very judgmental bitty, came outside right after her and did the same thing: Looked directly at her, snubbed her nose and walked away. Wow! What a greeting! Nice people he works with, she thought.

Then Noah came walking out. Ali took one look at him and realized the fat skanky blonde must be Christine because she was definitely acting like a jealous girlfriend.

What was really going on between them, she wondered.

Ali got out of her four-wheel drive and into his sleek, sexy, silver sports car. She couldn't believe how attractive he was and that he even had a car to match. She was floored, or should I say enamored. He was so adorable! Just like a cute puppy. A little guy who stood only five foot six inches on a good day and about one hundred fifty-five pounds, but he was well built and looked so handsome in his stylish white collar clothes, she thought. Just a typical nice long sleeved, button down shirt with dress pants and shoes. It wasn't so much what he was wearing, but how he filled it out. His hair was dark and curly, but cut very short and neat, and to her, he had the most beautiful hazel green eyes ever.

They went to a Japanese restaurant not too far from his job. Ali, who was actually intimidated by a man for the first time in years, one who was actually ten years younger than she, ordered a single salmon handroll and could hardly get it down, because she couldn't stop staring at him long enough to eat it, as he was sitting directly across from her, making her feel very uncomfortable.

After they had lunch, he drove her back to her Jeep and went back inside the building, only to be hounded by all of his co-workers who insisted that he stole her away from Eli and became very angry with him.

The truth was, Christine didn't like Noah to be with a beautiful girl and found any excuse she could find to justify her anger with him. That situation is still up for debate, even to this day.

Noah kept calling her to talk to her for endless hours, but didn't want to hang out with her in person because he said he didn't want to piss off the people at his work any more or hurt his friend Eli.

He kept telling her that she wasn't his type. He didn't like all of her tattoos and she was too old for him. Ali just wanted to get that feeling again that she got when he was near her. She got such a warm, exciting feeling inside of her every time they spoke, and she wanted more. She knew he must have been feeling it too or he wouldn't have been staying on the phone with her as long as he had been.

Neither one of them wanted to hang up and break the connection, so sometimes they would just fall asleep together while still on the phone. After she heard his breathing and knew he was out, she would go ahead and hang up.

She continued going to her classes in Montclair, and afterwards she would call him. Sometimes he would call her while she was there, but it would completely distract her. She kept telling herself that no guy was ever going to come between her and her college education ever again.

But then, a few weeks after their first date, he told her one night that she could meet him at some club called the Bomber Squad in Fairfield. Ali jumped at the offer and drove right over there after she had finished her classes. He was there with a few of his guy friends who seemed like your typical white-collar yuppie businessmen. All of them seemed well mannered and clean-cut. Not like the guys she was used to being around when she was growing up.

She had a couple Heinekens with him and they all sat around in plastic chairs out in the back courtyard talking. Noah introduced her to all his friends and they had a nice time.

Then when it came time to leave, all his friends went home. It was just Ali and Noah inside the romantically dim-lit club with the music playing and the energies flowing. The ambiance was perfect and they were both drawn to each other like two magnets and kissed for the first time. It was the first time Ali had kissed anyone in a very long time and it was breathtaking. He kissed her better than she ever imagined. So gentle, yet deep and passionate. He seemed as love- starved as she was.

She left her car at the club and drove with him to his condo that he shared with two other male roommates. He took her by her hand, leading her right into his bedroom, closing the door behind and finishing what they had started.

> Whisper to me
> Whisper in my ear
> Touch me gently
> Say the things I want to hear
> Then hold me closely
> Caress your body against mine
> Let me absorb you
> Deep into the channels of my mind
> Until the end of time.

By Ali

Making love to him was like a symphony beneath the sheets, every move as if it were choreographed in some grand dance, naked. Never in her life had she ever been so in synced with another lover as she was with him. She wanted to tell him, that very night, how much in love she was with him, but she knew he would think it was way too soon and most likely get turned off by it.

For the next three months, that scene would repeat itself over and over again, the passion never once letting up or fading away. They would come together every single time they made love. He inspired her and captivated her and the more she fell into him, the more he would try pushing her away, afraid of his own feelings getting out of control. But she wanted them out of control, so she could let hers go with his together.

He was sometimes cruel and would tell her not to come over, that he didn't want to see her anymore. He would say it was over. But then, she'd get a call at three in the morning, to pick him up in the city, because his friends had abandoned him there. They would go back to his place, he'd apologize to her for hurting her feelings, and they would make love all over again until the sun came up.

Every time felt like it was the first time. She would do anything for him and he knew it. No one ever brought her to climax the way he did.

He was a player and she was intrigued. No one was as good a player as she was, but she wasn't playing him. She actually had genuine feelings for him that she never thought she'd ever feel again. But she knew he was young and she had never been with a younger guy before in her entire life and she enjoyed his challenge. He would say things that would hurt her, but then make love to her like she was a goddess.

In her mind, he was her boy toy. In his mind, she was the forbidden older woman that everyone he knew warned him about. She was not the marrying kind, but who was thinking marriage when there was so much sexual passion between them?

She loved watching him lie naked next to her. She would

follow every curve and every muscle with her eyes while caressing them with her hands. His soft, young flesh that always had the scent of some masculine man soap. She couldn't resist putting her mouth on his swollen member, his perfectly shaped love shaft, that she could feel pulsing deep inside her throat as she gently sucked it in.

Then, before she got too carried away, she would stop and take it out. Driving him crazy wanting it more. He would make it last, he had incredible control. Neither one of them took any precautions of what might happen when they were finished, but the thought did cross their minds on several occasions that she might get pregnant. They swore each time that they would be more careful the next time. But to feel his hot flesh inside of her, caused her to tighten her legs around his body in a grip that forced his explosion to penetrate her entire being, causing her to open up like a Venus fly trap and close around him like he was some harmless, innocent prey she had just captured.

Making Love

Close your eyes and drift into fantasy.
Feel the emotions
Together just you and me.
Exploring the deepest channels of ecstasy.
Exchanging the fluids and mixing the chemistry.
Allowing your strength to absorb deep inside of me
Knowing I'm wanting you just like your wanting me.
Exploding like magic, creating an energy
A powerful surge of love
Flowing endlessly
Naked.

By Ali

And then it happened...

She was late getting her monthly. She stopped at the CVS pharmacy on her way to college to pick up a pregnancy test.

When she got to school, before she went into her classroom, she went directly into the ladies room to pee on the stick.

Oh my God! She thought

"Oh shit! Now what am I going to do? I can't get an abortion, he's Jewish. I can't kill a Jew or I'll be like Hitler. The Jews are the chosen ones!" she said aloud to herself.

Ironically, she had been complaining to her friend Eli for the past two years that she wanted another Jewish child. He asked her if he could assist her, but she thought he meant with getting her pregnant with his child. She thought he was way too old and with all the medication he was taking, the child would be born mutated. She declined his offer with a "thanks but no thanks."

Who knows, maybe he introduced her to Noah so he could give her what she'd been wanting for so long. After all, he was a dear friend and wanted to see her happy.

Adam and Tyler had a Jewish father. She loved the Jewish people. Her ancestors were Jewish.

This was an unexpected surprise, and she didn't know what she should do next. She was thankful that she wasn't still on parole any longer and thought that she might actually be able to keep her baby.

She would have to call the Department of Youth and Family Services as soon as possible to find out. Either way, she wasn't going to abort it. She was way too superstitious for that.

She wondered if she was too old at thirty-nine to have another child, but thought about all the other women who had given birth much older than that with no complications, so she put it out of her mind.

She now had to inform her lover. That should be fun! She thought

She was way too excited to keep it a secret until then, so she informed her class of the new discovery and everyone seemed genuinely happy for her.

After class, she called Noah and asked him if it would be Ok for her to come over. He didn't seem to mind too much, so she did. After they hung out in the living room with his roommates for a while, they went into his bedroom and closed the door.

She told him that she had to talk with him about something. He had no idea what it was pertaining to, but really didn't seem too thrilled about having what appeared to be a serious conversation with her at that time. He wasn't in the mood. "Oh well!" she thought. He really seemed annoyed that she was even there. She knew he really didn't want a serious relationship with her. She had only been some sexy older woman fantasy he had been fulfilling. She knew he thought it was becoming too much and wanted a break from it.

She sensed his distance and wasn't going to push herself onto him any longer. If he needed space, she would give him all the space in the world. But, only after she informed him that he was going to be a father. Or should I say, the unwilling sperm donor to her new project of motherhood?

So, as she was preparing to leave, realizing the rejection that would follow, she told him.

His response, as he sat at the edge of his bed, was to put his face down into his hands and moan out "Oh no, my life is ruined!" Then he continued with... "You *are* going to get an abortion aren't you? Aren't you too old to be having a child anyway? Doesn't this have to be both our decisions? Well I don't want it, so you either have to abort it or give it up for adoption."

Then he tried to bargain with her. "If you don't get the abortion, we are over and I won't see you any longer. But if you do get the abortion, I'll continue to see you, but I want to see other women as well."

He kept repeating over and over to her, "I don't want to be a father."

She took it that what he was really implying was that he enjoyed having great sex with her, but he didn't want her to be the mother of his child.

She was not the kind of woman he would ever bring home to meet his parent's, the same parents who had not envisioned their only biological child having offspring with someone like her.

She laughed at his pathetic attempts to get himself out of their predicament. Then replied, "Let's get this straight. You want me to trade the life of my unborn child for a few more throws in the sack with you?" He was an obvious player, who had absolutely no respect for any woman's feelings. "You're forgetting all the hours of conversations and the stories of your emotional abuse to your ex-girlfriends that you told me about." she continued

"Not to mention your attempts to do the same to me. If I wasn't already so jaded, you may have actually done some permanent damage to my psyche. But I can tune you out just as well as I have tuned you in.

God should punish you by giving you your own little girl to worry about. And here's a clue, daddy, I won't tell anyone in your circle about my pregnancy, so you won't have to worry that your married boss or your co-workers will find out anything, as long as you don't tell them. But, I'm going to have my baby with or without your consent! As for seeing you any longer, this relationship is officially O*V*E*R! Have a good evening and please do not bother calling me any longer! You made it perfectly clear that you do not want to be a father to my child, so good-bye!"

She closed the door behind her and walked out of his life. Temporarily!

Chapter 33

Ali began her prenatal care at the clinic at St. Joseph's Hospital on Main Street in Paterson. When they took down her history, she had informed them of her family being from Quebec, Canada. They seemed concerned and sent her for genetic testing immediately after.

Apparently, there we're a small sect of European Jews who excessively inbred hundreds of years ago to the point of creating a genetic mutation or disease called "Tay-Sachs."

She had three other children in this lifetime, and yet, this was the first time she was hearing about some gene or genetic mutation that there was a chance she could be carrying.

Then, to her surprise, she actually tested positive for it.

"You've got to be kidding me!" she said to them. "So what exactly does this mean?"

"Well, nothing if the father of your child tests negative, but if he doesn't and he tests positive, there's a ninety-nine percent chance that your child will develop the disease and die before the age of six."

"You've got to be kidding me. " She said again. "Holy crap!"

They told her that the gene was prevalent in Ashkenazi Jews. Noah just happened to be Ashkenazi.

She had promised herself that she would leave the boy alone and not bother him with her pregnancy, but this was a matter of life or death, and not theirs, but her fetus's.

So, she sucked up her pride and called him. She told him that she needed him to go get a blood test downtown at the hospital, that she had tested positive for the Tay-Sachs gene and needed to know if he carried the same gene. He insisted he did not have any disease and would not go anywhere to be tested for one. She angrily replied "Idiot! It is not that you have a disease. It's a gene, stupid little man! And you WILL go get tested or I will send every one of your co-workers an e-mail informing them of your little secret."

ON THE DAY OF HIS appointment, Noah picked Ali up at her house so she could go with him. He had no idea where to go and she wanted to make sure that he got there and had it done.

It had been a few weeks since they had seen each other, and the tension was very thick between them. The ride was extremely quiet and in the office, she thought to her self, "What have I done to this poor guy? He's so young and so innocent, even though he doesn't think so." He didn't look like he belonged with her. He seemed like some nice, young Jewish guy who should be dating some nice, young innocent Jewish girl, not some overly experienced ex-con, ex-stripper. She actually felt sorry for him that day and hated being cruel to him, but she knew if she didn't threaten him, he wouldn't have gotten involved.

Turns out that he tested negative and her fetus was in the clear and good to go.

She thanked him for being cooperative and asked him if he would like to go with her to an ultrasound that she had scheduled for that same day.

For the first time, he had gotten to see what the fetus looked like inside of her. His daughter! Again he insisted that he didn't want to be a father and they left it at that.

She didn't bother him again and he didn't call her either.

ALI HAD TO DROP OUT of college two semesters shy of getting her degree. The weather was cold and the ice that had formed on the roads was so slippery that she almost fell on several occasions and was too afraid of hurting herself while walking to her classes to continue.

She was very tired most of the time and had the worst heartburn ever imaginable. She had to sleep on eight pillows practically sitting up at night, because when she leaned back ever so slightly, the pain would cut through her like a dagger. Antacids didn't work at all; they had only made things worse.

Ali's ex-sister-in-law, Laurie, kept her company practically her entire pregnancy, talking to her on the phone while they both stayed in bed. Laurie was living in Florida by Ali's family and she had gained so much weight that she couldn't even walk and had to get around in a wheelchair.

She still smoked cigarettes after being diagnosed with emphysema and would remove the oxygen tube from her nose in order to take a drag from it. Ali had asked her why she had killed herself. She told her that she didn't want to live any longer without her brother, who had married another woman after they had had their daughter. "That's crazy!" she told her. "He's such an abusive dirt bag, why would you even bother thinking about him? He beats his wife constantly and even sold his twins to some diamond merchants for a car." Ali had disowned her brother after that.

Laurie was only two years older than she was and loved when Ali would read to her from the book of poetry she was writing about Noah. It was like an endless love story that she looked forward to hearing about every time they spoke on the phone. Ali would try to write something everyday just so she could read it to her. They had become the best of friends again. Ali told her that she would bring the baby down to Florida after it was born so she could meet her new niece. It gave them both something to look forward to.

Chapter 34

~~~~~~~~~~~~~~~~~~~~~~~~~~~~~~~~~~~~~

Now in her sixth month, Ali had spent most of the winter home crocheting and doing Needlepoint's, just like she had done while she was incarcerated.

The doctor had told her to "Climb up on your perch like a bird and sit there until you hatch." She started having premature contractions and the doctors were worried she would have a premature birth.

She was a high-risk pregnancy, due to her age of thirty-nine.

So, she was forced to spend most of her time on her bed at home.

Eli would sometimes call her on the phone and ask her if she wanted to meet him at a diner. He would buy her dinner and they would talk for a while, then she would go back home to sit on her perch. He felt really guilty for introducing her to his co-worker who got her pregnant, and then abandoned her and her child, so he kind of felt obligated to at least make sure that she ate properly once in a while.

IT WAS THE BEGINNING OF March 2004 and the weather was nice, so she had taken a drive up route 23 to the crafts store Michael's to get herself some more yarn for the baby blankets she was working on.

She noticed that her gas gage was on E, so she stopped at an Exxon gas station north bound near the store. A very big man with long, dark, beautiful, thick, shiny hair, tied back into a ponytail, wearing glasses that made him look studious, came to her window and asked her "How much? Cash or credit?"

She couldn't help but notice his accent and that he was the same guy she had seen working across the highway, at the other Exxon southbound, a few months earlier when she had stopped for gas there.

She had noticed him then, and had actually gotten butterflies in her stomach from the sight of him standing there. She was extremely attracted to him, but thought to her self "He's probably a foreigner who can't even speak English and is most likely married with a bunch of kids." Even though he kind of looked like a college guy, she drove away not giving him another thought.

She was still subconsciously trying to get over her baby's father.

But it had been many months without a word from him and she was very lonely.

She couldn't let herself drive away this time, without at least trying to make some kind of contact with him, so when he came to her window to collect the money, she asked him where he was from.

He told her Istanbul, Turkey. "Be still my heart! Dracula!" she cried out as she put her hands together over her bosom. "I love Istanbul!" she continued. "Constantinople is where they hung Dracula's head after he was killed by a Turk. Are you Muslim?" she asked. "Yes," he replied. "She told him how Dracula's father had belonged to the Order of the Dragons, a small group of rich guys who fought against the Turks to keep their religion out of his kingdom. She was completely fascinated with Dracula and now she was completely fascinated with him, who reminded her of Dracula.

He told her his name was Aydin, and that he had come to America two and a half years before to learn English so he could take his TOFEL exam to get into the Istanbul university and become a professor of Fifteenth Century, Ottoman Empire written Language. He already had his Masters degree in that subject. "Wow," she thought, "This guy is so smart and he's pumping gas like some poor, uneducated loser."

It's so true that you can't judge a book by its cover. She

couldn't stop talking with him and sat in her car by the gas pump for at least an hour. He told her that she was the first English-speaking person, since he got here, that actually had a conversation with him.

He told her that all the other English-speaking people, who had money, thought they were too good for his company.

"What a shame!" she thought. She asked him where he was living and he told her Paterson. He also told her that he hadn't gotten the chance to visit anywhere else in this country and was going back to Turkey in December when his passport expired. He had to go into the Turkish Army for a year as part of his citizenship there. He was thirty years old and wasn't married nor was he a father to any children.

She couldn't believe that someone had been visiting her country, living in Paterson and had never even seen a play on Broadway in New York City. It's not like it was a hundred miles away. She figured that pumping gas wasn't a very lucrative job, so he probably couldn't afford to waste his money on that kind of entertainment.

So Ali asked him if he would like to go to the city to see a play with her, that it would be her treat. He said he would like that. He told her that he would take off from work on Tuesday, which was six days later, as it was already Wednesday. She gave him her phone number and told him to call her to confirm their date.

Two days later, out of the blue, Ali got a call from Noah at one o'clock in the morning.

He told her that he had been drinking, but that he missed her so much and wanted her to come over to his place to visit.

She couldn't say no to him and went right over.

It was just like it used to be. Nothing had changed. He took her by the hand and gently led her into his bedroom, then closed the door. It was the first time she had felt like they were a family since it all began. He was hugging her protruding belly and kissing it as if he loved her and his baby all along.

They made gentle, quiet love, only this time, it was with tears streaming down her face as she released some of the pain she had pent up inside of her, that he had caused. They held onto each other tightly. She lay in his arms as he caressed her hair afterwards. She told him she loved him and he mirrored those words back to her.

In the morning she went back home. He told her he would call her, but he never did. He wouldn't even return her calls when she left messages.

He had mentioned that he had been seeing an intern at his job a few months earlier, but he told her, that he wasn't seeing her any longer. Her name was Trisha. He described her as having red hair and freckles and said that her pale skin turned him off and that she also had Halitosis, which made him gag whenever she wanted to kiss him.

Ali thought that it was good that none of his girlfriends satisfied him. She didn't want to hear how great his office romances were while she sat at home gaining weight and getting fat from his child. But to him, they were just friends now. To her, she was only concerned with her pregnancy and kept control of any jealous feelings, realizing that there was absolutely nothing she could do to change things, anyway.

> I've been searching forever
> To find genuine love.
> I've been waiting and wishing
> That soon that day would come
> The aching and longing I feel deep inside
> Makes me want to cry.
> I'd do whatever it takes if I were satisfied
> To be what I'm meant for
> A beautiful bride
> I want that feeling of love again inside
> I come so close
> But then that feeling dies.
>
> By Ali

Chapter 35

It was Tuesday morning, four days after Ali had spent the night with Noah.

She still hadn't heard from him.

The phone rang at 9 AM, waking her from her sleep.

"Hello?" she said, in a tired, wispy voice. "Ali?" the voice replied with a thick accent. "Aydin?" she asked as she immediately recognized it.

"Yes! Are we still going to the city today?" he asked

"Aydin, did you take the day off, just for me?"

"Of course!" he replied

"Oh shit!" she thought. She had completely forgotten about their date. He was supposed to call her to confirm it, but he hadn't. He probably misunderstood what she had said to him.

Oh well, its no problem!

She wasn't scheduled to do anything that day anyway, and it would be fun to get out to the city and walk around.

"I guess we're going to the city today! I'll come pick you up." She told him.

She actually got excited thinking about it. A day in the city with her newly found, sexy Turkish friend. That should be fun! And he was a Muslim, she'd have to get a Koran and read it if she wanted to get to know him better. He had told her during their first conversation that he went to a Mosque every Friday faithfully and didn't eat pork or drink alcoholic beverages. Wow, just like the Jews. She thought.

She picked him up in front of his apartment on Getty Ave,

only four miles from her home, and drove them straight into the city from route 80 over the George Washington Bridge. It was something she loved to do and wished she could do more often. She just didn't like going into the city alone and didn't have very many friends to go with her, if any.

She knew that the Lincoln Tunnel would have been a lot faster to get them to where they were going, but she got claustrophobic driving in tunnels.

She wanted to take him to all her favorite places. First, they would park by Canal Street, then they would walk around and see all the colorful things in the little shops and eat on Mulberry Street in her favorite Italian restaurant Sorentino's. They made the best, stuffed artichokes she'd ever had. She was sure he had never tasted one before and she was right. He had never even heard of them.

It was really exciting to introduce him to new food. She had to teach him how to eat it. A finger food that you peeled off one leaf at a time and scraped the meat with your teeth. Then, finally, getting to the heart was the best part. He really seemed to enjoy it. And the olive oil and garlic breading was amazingly orgasmic! Then came the main courses of rigatoni in vodka sauce for her and meatballs in spaghetti for him. What great selections!

He insisted on paying, even thought it was her treat to take him out. "I am the man and I pay!" he said in a stern, Turkish voice. She didn't want to offend his manhood or insult his custom, so he got no arguments from her.

She had kept her pregnancy a secret, and covered herself in baggy clothes that concealed it from him, thinking that he might not want to hang out with a pregnant woman if she had told him right away.

After they had eaten dinner, they began walking towards the theater district. After walking only a short distance, she began getting bad stomach cramps and had to stop for a minute.

It was the perfect opportunity for that first kiss. He held her gently in his arms, and while gazing down into her eyes, put his mouth against hers. For a second it took her breath away, but then, he lost control, becoming too aggressive with his passion and he bit her lip, hard! "Owe!" she cried, "That hurts!" Was he a vampire trying for blood? She thought

She decided it was time that she let him know why she wasn't up to walking as fast as he was. She said to him, "Aydin there's something I need to tell you. I'm actually six months pregnant." His face suddenly lit up like a child on Christmas morning.

He gently put his arm around her shoulder and assisted her in every step she took. It was actually really very sweet. He instantly became protective of her and her unborn baby. Not the reaction she had expected.

They walked all the way to the theaters from Mulberry Street. Ali had become very chilled from the temperature change as the sun went down, so they stopped at a maternity store, that just happened to be on their path, and he bought her a beautiful, thick, hooded, white, zip up sweater to keep her warm. He was such a nice, considerate guy!

When they got to the theaters, she noticed that "Wicked" was playing. She asked him if he wanted to see that one. She explained that it was about the Wizard of Oz, before the characters were grown-up. He had never even heard of the Wizard of Oz before.

Now she was really intrigued by him. He was like some alien from another planet. I mean, who has never heard of "The Wizard of OZ" she thought. It's amazing!

She spent the next fifteen minutes catching him up on the story, so he would at least be familiar with the characters in the play. She bought them their tickets and they went inside. The show started at 8PM and ended at 11 o'clock.

He sat next to her and held her hand the entire time. She couldn't help but notice how he kept caressing her with his thumb. She couldn't believe how affectionate he was, like a gentle giant. He was six foot-two and two hundred and forty pounds.

He really enjoyed the play and so did she. They walked all the way back to her Jeep afterwards and it took a couple of hours. He kept asking her along the way if she was tired and wanted to catch a taxi, but it was such a perfect evening with him that she just didn't want it to end.

They didn't get back to the parking garage until after one-thirty in the morning. Her car was the only one left in the lot, which had already closed.

She just stood there staring at her lonely little truck that had been abandoned by all the other vehicles. "Oh NO!" she cried. She was too tired from all the walking, and suddenly realized how much she longed to lie down and rest.

The street was so empty and the city so dark and quiet, and there were no taxi's around for them to take out of there.

She tried not to panic, but carefully explained to him, so he would understand, that she didn't have a spare key, so she wasn't going to be able to get them back home until the parking garage reopened in about seven hours.

She felt so responsible. She should have paid more attention to the time, but thought the garage would be open all night.

He was being so understanding. He just took her by the hand and led her down the road. They kept walking back towards the theater district until they finally found an available cab.

When they got inside, he told the driver to take them to the Port Authority Bus Terminal.

Suddenly she realized that he actually knew how to get around the city with the mass transit system, something she was clueless about.

Before long, she was sitting next to him on a bus heading back to Paterson. She had her head on his shoulder, with her eyes closed, and his comforting arms around her. And to her astonishment, he began to softly sing some Turkish lullabies in her ear.

WHEN SHE GOT BACK TO Paterson, she called me to come pick her up. The next morning, I drove her back to his apartment, where they caught a bus back to New York so she could get her truck,

Again, he insisted on paying for it. Ali knew he worked hard for the little money that he made and she respected him for that, but she didn't want to take advantage of his generosity and felt very uncomfortable about it.

SEVERAL DAYS LATER, SHE BEGAN visiting him at night at the gas station. She enjoyed watching him work, even if it was something as simple as pumping gas and collecting the money. He would educate her on his religion and his customs and she desired to be like him, a gentle Turkish Muslim with a Masters degree. How intriguing!

She couldn't understand why so many people hated the Muslims and called them all terrorists because of a few fanatics. How Fucking Ignorant!!! She was so tired of the world with their DAMN prejudices. What the fuck is wrong with people! She thought. Not everyone who is Muslim is a terrorist. Then she thought about all the innocent people who had been killed as heretics by the Catholic Church. More people than Hitler killed in the Holocaust. Christians can be just as fanatical about killing those they hate or fear than any other religion.

Why can't people just admit that if they want to hate and kill someone, they should hate and kill themselves, for failing to be good, kind, loving and compassionate human being's. Why hate others because they're not like you!

If Ali had any prejudices, it was against "stupid, ignorant, biased people who think that they are above everyone else in this world." She HATES people like that.

Chapter 36

Over a week had gone by, and she became very angry that she hadn't heard a word from Noah after the incredible night they shared.

She woke me up extremely early on Monday morning, complaining about the way Noah had been treating her. She told me that she was going over to his condo to confront him when he left for work. She said, "If he wants to treat me like a whore, then I want to be paid like one. He owes me two hundred dollars for Friday night and I'm going to collect it from him!" And off she went in her little Sahara Jeep.

She parked in the lot facing his building so she could catch him leaving. She told herself that he better walk out with some beautiful woman or she would have absolutely no respect for him.

If he had a woman with him, then his not returning her calls would make sense. If not, that would just mean he was a weirdo with major head problems.

She sat there for two hours and watched his roommates leave first. She ducked down in her seat so that they wouldn't notice her and tip him off.

Then, she saw him coming out soon after. And sure enough, he was with a tall, thin, fashionably dressed, gorgeous redhead. "Good for him!" she thought

She was actually proud that her lover had such defined taste in women and didn't mind the competition.

Wearing a thick winter coat, so her pregnancy wouldn't be noticed, Ali jumped out of the vehicle to confront them.

She was cool and calculating, not like any other **normal** pregnant woman would be who just caught her lover with another female. She wasn't surprised in the least, but she wanted the money she felt was due her for compensation to make things even.

"You must be Trisha." she said "Noah and I have some business we need to discuss, don't we Noah?" Trisha told him that she would be waiting by her car and walked across the lot, far enough away so she couldn't hear their conversation.

Ali just looked at him with disgust. He had lied to her and she hated liars. He had told her it was over with that girl.

She repeated to him what she had said to me. "You want to treat me like a whore, I want to be paid like one. You owe me two hundred dollars and I've come to collect."

"What?" he said in surprise. "I'm not paying you two hundred dollars! I don't even have it. I don't carry that kind of cash around with me." he continued

"That's Ok, I take checks, credit cards, whatever you have." she replied

"You're out of your mind and I'm not paying you!" he said again

"Then I'm going to tell your girlfriend where you were Friday night" and she waved her hand, motioning for her to come back over to them while she yelled "TRISHA?"

Noah began to panic. "Ok! I'll pay you, but I can't right now, can you wait until lunch and I'll meet you?"

It was too late for her to respond. His girlfriend was already standing next to them again.

Ali felt the need to explain why she had just called her over, so she said, "Noah has an addiction problem, don't you Noah? He owes me some money and I've come to collect it." Trisha looked over at him with impatience and disgust; she just wanted to get to work and didn't want to be involved in his nonsense, and said, "Have some respect for me already." Ali sneered at those words and responded, "You want HIM to have respect for a woman? You're kidding, right?"

Trisha just gave up and walked to her car to wait for him.

Noah told Ali to wait there while he went to console his girlfriend. Then, he walked over to his own car and returned with a check made out to cash for two hundred dollars.

She said to him as she was getting in her jeep to leave, "It better not bounce." He was insulted by her words, and insisted that his check was good. "It better be!" she yelled out her open window as she drove away, leaving him to stand alone in the parking lot.

She drove straight to the bank around the corner from Noah's condo complex and immediately signed and cashed the check. As she drove back home, Ali pondered on what had just happened. A part of her felt guilty that she had just taken money from him. All she ever wanted to do was give to him.

But another small part of her was glad that she had gotten even without actually having to hurt him for satisfaction.

Later on that same evening, she took a ride to Toys R' Us to purchase a stroller and a car seat with the money. They were the only items her baby girl would receive from her father, and not given willingly; it had been forced.

While Ali walked around the store, she received an unexpected phone call from him, informing her that his drama queen girlfriend had gone into work that morning, crying hysterically to her co-workers and boss, that he had betrayed her with another woman. They all took her side against him and ruined his day.

The owner of the company got wind of the situation and informed everyone in the office, the following week, that office romances were now prohibited. Anyone caught violating the new rule would be fired.

That was just fine with Ali. Maybe now Noah would keep his pecker in his pants long enough to actually get to know someone before he screwed her!

Noah actually thanked Ali for helping him get rid of his problem. He had been trying for months, so he claimed, but didn't have the balls to tell her to her face that he didn't want to be with her any longer. What a coward!

"Better luck next time!" she told him. "Imagine how Trisha

would have felt had she known I was carrying your child inside of me." Then he thanked her for not squealing on him.

She told him about her new boyfriend from Istanbul, and without trying to rub it in his face, or maybe she was, not that she thought he might actually care anyway, she let him know that she was really attracted to Aydin, and told Noah to leave her alone.

Chapter 37

He only had nine months left, before he had to go back home. His passport would expire on December 13, 2004.

It seemed a long way off, but the thought was always in the back of her mind that he'd be leaving her someday.

She thought about the two and a half years that he had already spent here in The States and wished he could have spent that time with her. If only she had met him sooner. It was their fate. He told her he didn't believe in "ASK", which he said, in his language, meant "True Love".

She spent the next three months sitting in her car from 6 pm until 11 pm at the gas station, when he was working.

When he wasn't pumping gas, he would sit next to her and they would converse. She corrected his poor English to help him and enjoyed listening to him telling stories of his life in Istanbul and the villages back home. She was enamored with his Turkish accent.

She loved the way he pronounced "Probably"! "Propobably." She even began saying that whenever she had to use that word in a sentence.

He became her fantasy vampire, and she was thankful that she had somewhere to go in the evenings, a reason to get out of the house.

She volunteered to drive him home every night so he wouldn't have to take the bus, as he didn't have a license. She would park on the side street and they would hug and kiss and hold each other.

They were both comforted by their companionship. He was

very lonely and missed his home and she was very lonely and wished she could go back with him *to* his home.

But he was a Muslim and she was a not even close to being perfect Jew. Even if she wasn't Jewish, his family would never approve because she was different. As he had once said to her "Your ways are not my ways!" in a voice that sounded just like Bela Lugosi's.

She had brought the DVD "The Wizard of Oz" for him to watch, and after he had watched it, he told her that the moral of the story was "There's no place like home." It had really made him homesick to see that flick. She felt so bad for him. He was like an alien from a far away planet, missing his own people.

She made him souvenirs to take back home with him so he would always remember her. She crocheted him a blanket, painted his portrait on canvas with acrylic paints and began taking lots of photos for an album she would give to him right before he left.

He would fill her tank with gas, wash her car while she sat in it on the days he wasn't too busy, and put oil in her car when it was low. He even gave her food to eat from inside the mini-mart when she was hungry.

If ever there was love in this world, they felt it for each other. But he didn't believe in love, and she didn't believe that he didn't love her.

Eternal Sounds

Close your eyes and sing to me
A symphony of harmony
Tell me how you'll always be
There, for me to feel complete
Show me now a way to see
Beyond the pain and misery.
My love for you will never die
No matter when we end our lives
So dream with me a fantasy
To set us free from all the grief
And sore with me beyond the clouds
An endless flight of eternal sounds.

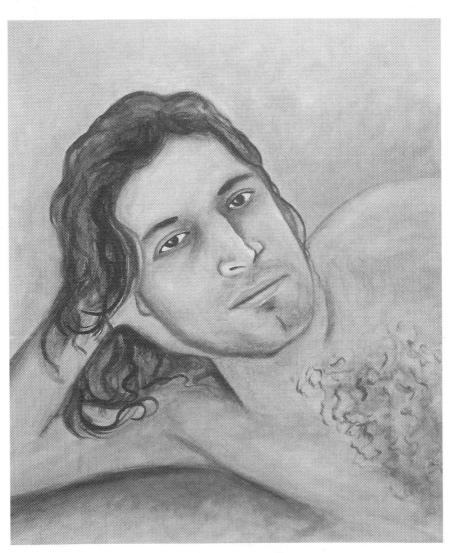

Painting of Aydin

Chapter 38

Then it happened...
Ali went into labor a day before her due date in June of 2004.

Her daughter, Amanda, had come to the hospital that morning to witness the birth of her baby sister, but the labor lasted all day, and by 5 PM, she was tired of waiting and wanted to go home to eat.

She told her mother to call her when her water broke. But it never did, and the doctor sent her back home, thinking it was false labor.

Later that night, around midnight, Ali jumped up out of bed while I was in the bathroom getting ready to go out with my friends to party, and yelled, "If I don't get to the hospital NOW, I'm going to have this baby in my bed."

She thought about the bloody mess that it would make on her clean, white comforter, and refused to let that happen.

She insisted on driving herself to the hospital, but wanted me to go with her. Thank God I didn't hang out with my friends that night, or I would have missed something incredible.

She had to pull over twice on the way, when she had contractions. Each time, I would ask her if I could drive, but she insisted on doing it her self.

It had become a challenge for her, when a nurse at the hospital, told her that she would have to call an ambulance when it came time to have her baby. The nurse said the pain would be too intense and that she wouldn't be able to drive herself. Ali wanted to prove her wrong, but also prove to her self that she could handle the pain of childbirth yet again.

After we got to the hospital, I began yelling to a security guard to get her a wheelchair. By then, she was hanging onto a fence, unable to walk any farther to the building. As soon as we got inside, a nurse immediately pushed her into an elevator to take her upstairs to the labor and delivery ward. She was fully dilated by the time she got out of her clothes, into a robe, and onto a bed.

Within minutes they were breaking her water and she was giving birth in the delivery room. They had told her it was too late for any medication, but she wouldn't have taken anything anyway. All her children were natural births and this one was no different.

She really wanted Amanda to be there, but it was too late.

I was allowed to be with her and actually assisted in the delivery. She never screamed, but the pain in her face was like nothing I had ever seen in her before. The doctor kept telling her to breathe because she was holding her breath. They told me to keep the oxygen mask on her face, but what good was that if she wasn't breathing?

And then I saw it! It looked like a floppy gray doll coming out of her. It was the most incredible sight I had ever seen. This thing that didn't even look real, literally coming out of her.

For a second, I felt sorry for her, because I thought it was dead, a stillborn. It was like some rubbery toy covered in gray goo. I instinctively put my finger out to it and said "Hey, little one" and it took its first breath of life grabbing hold of my finger. The warm, wet feel of its flesh was so strange and yet exciting and overwhelming at the same time. It had come to life right before my very eyes.

I was the first human to ever touch it. The doctor and the nurses were all wearing gloves, so they didn't count.

They said "It's a girl!" then carried her over to an area to clean her off and wrap her in a receiving blanket. Then they handed her over to me, thinking I was her father.

I was actually holding this newly created delicate human

life in my arms. Her mother was still on the table with her eyes closed, trying to deal with the traumatic pain.

I didn't want to bother her, after all that she had just gone through, so I sat down in a chair and waited for her to recover. When I saw that her eyes were open again and that she was alert, I walked her little girl over to her and gently placed her in her arms. She looked at her warm and beautiful bundle of joy and cried, "I can't believe I did it again! I actually created another baby!" It was a blessed miracle!

I thanked Noah in my mind, for not wanting to be there to experience this, because if he had been, I would have missed out on this incredible life altering experience. Never again would I look at children the same way.

Randy and Sophia

Chapter 39

Ali wanted Sophia's father to come see his baby girl, but she thought there was nothing she could do to get him there. He had made it perfectly clear, time and time again, that he wanted nothing to do with either of them.

She wanted her daughter to at least have her father's last name. She didn't want to make the same mistake that she had made with her first child, by giving her newborn another man's name, that wasn't even her father. And, anyway, Ali didn't even like her last name.

She called Noah and told him that his child had been born, but before she could leave the hospital with her, the baby had to be given a name. He said he didn't care what she named her. Ali asked him if he would come to the hospital to sign her birth certificate so she could at least have his last name. Of course he adamantly refused. What else would you expect?

So she asked him if he would mind if she called his mother to ask her how she might feel, about her son not giving her only biological granddaughter his family's last name.

He took it as a threat and said he would be right there.

She was so thrilled that she was going to be able to show off their new creation. But when he got to the hospital, to her disappointment, Noah didn't even want to see his own child. Ali said "Noah, look at her, isn't she beautiful?" He looked away and responded with, "She's ugly! All babies are ugly!" and he ran out, just as quickly as he could *after* signing the birth certificate.

"Well, at least she has a Jewish name. I can't wait until the Rabbi gives her, her Hebrew name. I don't think I'll be inviting his family to the ceremony, though" she said to me after I got to the hospital to bring her and Sophia home.

As SOON AS SHE GOT out of the hospital, she was right back at the gas station showing off her beautiful newborn to her Turkish boyfriend. Even if her own Jewish father denied her, her temporary Muslim father welcomed her with open arms. He was like a proud, doting father and he adored his newly pretend daughter.

It was the most incredible memory they had made together, watching him read the children's book "Little Bear" to her, in his Turkish accent. As soon as Ali heard him, she burst out laughing hysterically. Imagine Dracula himself, reading a baby book to a newborn.

It was the sweetest thing she had ever seen. How could she not fall in love with a man like him? But he was leaving them. She always hoped in the back of her mind, that he would stay. She told him that if he married her, he could get his citizenship here in America. But he wasn't interested in staying. He was on a mission, and she was not part of the plan. She "propobably" loved him even more because he was leaving.

He would drive her crazy every time she pulled up at the gas station to visit him. The first thing he would do was to pull Sophia's socks off her feet. No matter how cold it would get outside, he didn't care. He had a baby foot fetish. He told her they were the cutest, tiniest toes he had ever seen and he just had to see them, every time she was with him.

Aydin with baby Sophia

For the next six months, Ali was on a mission, to show her alien friend some of the places in her country worth seeing, places outside of Paterson, New Jersey.

She was so proud to be the one who changed his perceptions of America.

She took him all the way down to The Keys in Florida.

He told her that he thought Miami was a small village, so she had to drive him all throughout the city to show him exactly how big it really was.

They stayed on South Beach for the night and had such an incredible time there together.

Ali took him to meet her family in Orlando and spent a couple days with them. She brought Sophia over to Laurie's house so she could finally meet her niece for the first and last time. Laurie died a few months later weighing 385 pounds.

She had been such a good friend.

Ali never knew many people in her life that she could truly call a friend, but Laurie was her friend. She couldn't believe how someone so nice, could do that herself, leaving behind such a beautiful daughter.

She thought to herself, "No one lives forever, and we only have a few short years to try to do the right things for our families. Sophia, Randy and Tyler are my family now and I will do my best to keep them happy and healthy."

She hasn't been to Florida to visit her other family since.

THE TRIP TO FLORIDA WAS the end of the rainbow for them.

After they returned to Paterson, he slept over her house that night, but not in her bed. That place was reserved for Sophia.

The next day, he removed his sandals from his feet and left them at the end of her driveway. He said it was a custom to do that, when that person was never going to return to that home again.

She gave him a great big hug and kiss good-bye, then drove him back to Getty Avenue and dropped him off in front of his apartment. She watched him out of her rearview mirror, with tears streaming down her face, as she drove off into the sunset.

She went back home and took his dirty, black, completely beat up, used, nasty sandals, with holes in them, back into her house and put them under her bed, then said to herself, "If it's destiny, he'll come back to me someday!"

She had given him her email address and asked him to email her when he got back home, and he had given her, his. He told her he would do that, but never did.

For the next year, she would check her emails every single day in hopes of hearing from him. She would send him emails and photos of Sophia, showing him how much she was growing.

He never responded, and she wasn't even sure he was getting them. But they were never returned to her as a delivery failure, so she assumed he must have been. For whatever reasons, he just wasn't responding to her. She figured he must have gone into the Army, but there had to have been a computer around.

She never gave up. Talk about persistence!

Fallen Sky

Chapter 40

Everyday, for months, Ali would check her emails to see if Aydin had written to her. After a while, she had decided it was time to move on and forget about him, but she just couldn't. She had tried to, so many times before, to get him out of her head.

He was the perfect doting father, the gentleman she had dreamed of marrying. He was all about family and reminded her that Sophia was her life and nothing else should ever take precedence over caring for her.

He told her once that she would lose her daughter if she went back to work. She already suspected that, and had no plans to do any such thing, that may distract her from paying full attention to her child. Sophia was her gift from God and knowing the evils that lurk in this world, she didn't know how long she would be able to keep her. "The Lord giveth and the Lord taketh away." She was going to spend every single moment with Sophia as if it were her last. She never knew when or what would happen to end it all, but she constantly lived with the fear that Sophia would be taken away from her.

She had gotten into a routine of breastfeeding on demand, with no set times for the feedings. She would bathe her everyday in a little blue tub that she set up on her bed and filled with water. She loved dressing her up in those cute little outfits for babies and taking photos of her.

Every single night, Ali would read to Sophia before she put her to sleep. She was not going to ever miss a chance to do that again. The loss of her other children still affected her after all those years. She was so horrified that something would happen again to this child, that she spent all of her time playing with her, keeping her content and over-protecting her. Sophia never left her sight unless Ali was in the shower. Even then, it was brief, as she hurried to get back to her. Although she had a beautiful white crib in her bedroom, Sophia would sleep in Ali's bed. The crib was pushed up against it as a guard to keep her from falling off.

Ali refused any vaccines for Sophia until she was a year old. She had read so many articles about the dangers of them. She wasn't going to put her child at risk so soon for complications. Sophia's pediatrician was so understanding of Ali's feelings and didn't push her at all to get them. He did have to inform her however, of the dangers of not having them, another two-edged sword? She thought I had moved out of the house with my girlfriend for the next couple of years and wasn't there as much as I had been before. I would still check in with her everyday, to see if she was fine, or if she needed something.

It's funny how people will accept a man and woman living together when they think that they're really family, but will get jealous and insecure when they think that your just roommates. We knew the game and played it well. We had been telling people for so long that we were cousins, to this day we still believe it, and no one comes between family.

NOAH WAS LIVING HIS LIFE with no responsibilities that came with being a father; Ali left him alone. Unfortunately, with no income coming in for her, she was forced to get assistance from the state, who, went after Noah to pick up the tab. But that took a while, so all was well and peaceful with her and his secret was safe, at least for a little while.

Until...

One day, six months after Sophia was born, Ali had taken a ride with her to Circuit City to check out camcorders. Aydin had only been gone for a couple of weeks. After Ali left the store and had driven back home, she got a call from Eli. "Did you talk to Christine at all today?" he asked. "Who?" she replied "Noah's boss, Christine. Did you see her at Circuit City and talk with her?"

"No. Why?"

Apparently, Christine had been in the store and had seen Ali with Sophia, and within fifteen minutes, everyone at Noah's job knew he had a child with her. She had told everyone that the child looked just like her father.

When Noah went into work the following day, everyone asked him if it was true and he admitted it. No one ever said another word about it to him after that. They were all in shock that he was a father and to Ali's child no less. Even Eli himself had kept his little secret from them.

Chapter 41

When Sophia was only six weeks old, Ali thought it would be nice if *she* had some nice Jewish grandparents, so she kind of caused herself a major headache, to say the least.

I don't know exactly what she was thinking at the time, I don't think she even knew, but she called Noah's mother to inform her, that she was a grandmother.

This was the first time she had ever spoken to someone in his family. When they were dating each other, he kept her a secret from them as well.

At first, his mother cried with joy that she was now a grandmother. But then, just as quickly as she had gotten excited about the news, her demeanor changed, and she became very defensive, questioning Ali's motive for calling. "How do you know it's his? Why did you call us? What do you want from us, we have no money? We want a DNA test before we'll even consider accepting her or getting involved." "Ok, so get the DNA test." Ali replied, "We're not paying for it, you pay for it!" she continued.

Ali got really upset, or should I say, **pissed off,** after realizing the mistake she had just made, by calling those people.

"Let's get this straight!" Ali replied, "You want me to pay for a DNA test to prove that Sophia is your sons child? You're out of your mind! I don't care what you think. I don't want anything from you people. How dare you insult me that way! I was just trying to be nice and let you know that you have your first biological grandchild. This was a big mistake calling you. Your fucking crazy!" and she handed me the phone.

I had been standing there quietly in the background, while she made the call. But after hearing her response, I realized that I was going to have to defuse the situation.

Ali was not very good at handling people who rejected her, or her child, for any reason. And she wasn't at all reluctant to let any one know how she really felt about him or her.

I spoke to Noah's mother and tried to calm everyone down. After that, Ali didn't hear from his family again. Not a good way to start a relationship, I thought.

Noah had gone over to Ali's house once to visit Sophia, shortly after his co-workers found out about his new fatherhood. Sophia was around seven months old by then. He had hoped to develop some paternal instincts for his daughter, but to no avail.

Ali noticed his pupils were dilated very small and thought he had taken something, accusing him of being high at the time. After having a long conversation with him when he got home, he admitted it to her, confirming her suspicions.

He told her that he had been taking Oxi-contins for a while, and had been on them when he was over there. He called himself a "Drug User", but insisted he was NOT a "Drug Addict". He told her that he could quit anytime he wanted. He just enjoyed getting high and didn't have a reason to quit. He was a grown man and could do what he wanted. If he wanted to get high, that was his right.

She agreed with his philosophy, but informed him, that she did not want Sophia around him while he was high. So, if he wanted to see her again, he would have to come over sober next time. Needless to say, that wasn't until Sophia's first birthday.

Noah claimed that he had no idea that Oxi-contins were an addictive opiate like heroin until Ali informed him. She always researched everything she could, about anything she could. She loved the Internet! Why he hadn't researched his own drug of choice, prior to putting it into his body, was another mystery to her. But, she thought that most men, when it came to stuff like that, were stupid anyway and it didn't surprise her in the least.

THEN...

A couple months before Sophia's first birthday, Noah called Ali to tell her he had purchased a DNA test online and wanted to come over to test Sophia. Ali let him do it. Together, they swabbed his mouth, then Sophia's, and sealed it in the pre-addressed manila envelope. Then, together they walked to the blue mailbox at the end of her street and dropped it inside.

Two weeks later Ali got a call from him informing her that the DNA tested positive and he was without a doubt, her father. Gee how surprising!

Then, out of the blue, Ali got another phone call from Noah's mother, asking if she would mind if her and her husband came over to meet their granddaughter. Ali invited them over for Sophia's first birthday. Noah had told her he wasn't coming, but Ali insisted that she wasn't going to have strange people, who she had never met before, coming into her house without him there, so he unhappily went along with them.

As soon as they arrived, she knew Noah was high again. "What an asshole!" she thought. His parents had brought Sophia a present and a card, but nothing from Noah. He never even brought his own daughter a birthday card, let alone a gift. He just sat there with a baseball cap covering his face so you couldn't see into his eyes and he didn't say a word the entire time he was there.

Ali took lots of photos with her camera. She figured it was a rare occasion and that it should be documented, and she was right. That was the first and last time Noah's parents were ever in Ali's house.

And then her nightmare began!

Chapter 42

It was a habit she had developed while in prison. Everyday, no matter what was going on, she would document her day in a datebook. For years, she kept a log of her daily activities. Not that it would matter to anyone else, she just needed something to look back on, to remind her of the things she did in her past or had to do in the future. Her short-term memory was often a problem, so she had to over compensate with a diary or calendar to remember events and days on which she had appointments. If something unusual happened, she would write it down.

She didn't even realize how important these documents would become, until the day she needed them as a reference for her defense.

Noah resented having to pay child support for a child he didn't even want. This was understandable. He especially resented having to give his hard-earned money to her. To him, Ali was an older woman unworthy of his affections and his money. More importantly to him, he had an addiction that he had to sustain and Oxi's were very expensive.

When the courts ordered him to pay child support, Noah refused. He was eventually brought before them **again** and was told that he had to come up with three thousand dollars that day or go to jail. His parents paid his way out of that situation. But then he decided to get cute with Ali, by calling and threatening to hurt her.

I can really sympathize with him, being a man and all, but Sophia was his child no matter how he would feel about it, and unfortunately for him, Ali would always be the mother of his child, no matter what he or anyone else thought of her.

Here are some of the things she had documented in her datebook...

June 2nd, 2005 Noah got back the DNA results that he was the father.

June 13, Sophia got her ears pierced by her doctor.

June 28th, Sophia's birthday party, Noah and his parents showed up.

July 1st, 2005, Noah went over to visit Ali and Sophia, than spent the night. He told her he loved her and then disappeared out of her life again for a while. How typical of him and how stupid of her to fall for his bullshit again! I guess she was just lonely and didn't care that he only wanted a piece of ass. I'm sure they didn't practice safe sex that night either. Was he trying to have another kid? Some people just don't learn!

August 27th, Ali's friend Laurie died.

October 29th, 2005, Noah came over to play with his daughter for hours, Ali suspected that he was high.

November 6th, 2005. Aydin finally emailed Ali for the first time since he left eleven months before. He told her that he had been in the army, stationed on an island off the coast of Greece and sent her a photo of him in his army uniform. His long hair had been cut short and he was looking better than ever.

They began using the webcam to communicate. Everyday they would tune in at the same time so that they could see each other. He got to see Sophia and thought she had grown so much. Ali was so happy to have him back in her life, even if he was thousands of miles away. She looked forward to seeing him everyday. November 30th, Aydin left for Istanbul from where he had been living in Turkey and lost communication with her for a while. She was alone again, until he contacted her. For the next few weeks, they communicated. Then, as suddenly as he appeared, he disappeared. Ali would only hear from him a few other times over the years, to let her know that he had been accepted into the University to get his PhD and to become a professor.

Who really knows what was going on in his life? For all she knew, he was married with children and cheating on his wife and kids behind her back, or maybe he wasn't. That is a mystery, she would never uncover. She eventually cleaned her bedroom and tossed out his old shoes. I guess it wasn't their destiny to be together after all.

November 14th, 2005, Ali took Sophia to the pediatrician for her vaccines, and the next day she was very sick. Four days later, she noticed her child having seizures, and took her to the neurologist who only had an appointment available for the 22nd. The doctor told her that the Petit Mar seizures we're not caused by the vaccines. Yeah right!

It was just a coincidence that she had gotten the vaccines right before the seizures. Picture that!

Ali had researched the vaccine she had been given that day, (DTaP), and she read that the seizures would last eighteen days. She had been observing her child the entire time, and that's exactly how long Sophia's seizures lasted. Eighteen days! Coincidence? There was not a chance in hell that she would allow her daughter to get the second vaccine!

What are these mandated vaccines really doing to those tiny, sensitive neurological systems of these poor, helpless newborns that can't refuse them? Parents really need to do their own research and stop taking the word of their doctors like they're gods and know everything, because they're NOT! They're human beings like everyone else and make mistakes that can cost someone their life. Just ask Michael Jackson's family.

Are doctors really that brainwashed by the pharmaceutical

companies, with their vaccines and medications, to think that parents are stupid enough not to know when something causes a reaction to their own children? Good God, this world is so fucking nuts!

Ali had thought that Sophia's father might have cared at least once that his infant daughter was sick, but he didn't care about anything that involved either of them. So she decided that it was high time to go to the courts on December 2nd to file for full custody of her daughter.

Why not? It shouldn't have even mattered to Noah, since he wasn't even concerned about her health.

But then, on December 8th, when he got the papers to go to court, Noah must have gotten so pissed off about everything that he completely snapped. He called her and threatened to kill her *and* Sophia. Ali just thought that the drugs had finally gone to his brain and made him go crazy.

Noah really sounded convincing that he was on his way over to her house to do whatever, so he wouldn't have to deal with her shit any longer.

Ali really didn't know him well enough to doubt his words and didn't want to take the chance. She immediately called 911 and told them that he was on his way over to kill her and her child. He never showed up, but they gave him a temporary restraining order that got dropped on the 16th because there was no proof. It was his word against hers. But he got arrested that same day. I don't know how that happened, but there was a pip hearing on January 11th and the courts granted him supervised visitations for 90 days on January 26th, 2005. Apparently her lack of credibility and her mental disability worked against her.

Five days later, Noah called DYFS (Department of Youth and Family Services) on her to get even. They sent investigators to check out her situation and his allegations. He had demanded that they take his child away from her mother, because she was, "a dangerous child molester" and he was concerned that "his daughter was in grave danger." After all, his baby girl was living with a convicted felon and a registered sex offender.

Ali had told the investigators about his threats and his supervised visitations, and they eventually left unconcerned.

This was only the beginning!

The fear that filled her when DYFS appeared at her house was pretty severe, but she kept her composure because she was confident that she was a good mother and knew that they would have to have a damn good reason this time to remove her child from her.

DYFS was not the same organization that had taken her other children away years ago, never to allow her to see them again until they were grown. They used to be known as the Gestapo, who would take children away from their parents for any reason to keep their grants going for the foster care program. But after years of complaints, they were restructured to be a more "family friendly" organization working to keep families together and provide help for them, instead of hurting them more.

Chapter 43

Noah's visitations began on February 17th, 2006 at the library on Main Street in Paterson.

Sophia greeted him with a kiss and the visit went well that day.

The following week, after the second visit, Noah called Ali, and she let him come over to her house the next day to visit her child without the court's supervision. He gave his baby girl a bath for the first time and told Ali that he had had an epiphany and realized that he wanted to be a father. She wasn't sure she believed him, but she was not going to deny her child the chance to have a father in her life, so she played along with him to see what would transpire.

Ali and Noah began seeing each other again and he spent more time with his daughter than he ever done before. He told Ali that he loved her and even asked her to marry him on March 11th, 2006.

He showed up at all of his supervised visitations and would even sleep over her house afterwards. Things were going well and she began trusting him more and more with their daughter. He wasn't doing drugs any longer and life was peaceful.

The courts granted him joint custody with her consent and he agreed to pay half for her daycare. He would get Sophia every other weekend. He had moved in with his parents and they helped him. Ali enrolled in the Massage Therapy Academy in Lodi, and Sophia began attending Kids University (a daycare/ preschool). Life was calm for some time. But Noah

NEVER helped Ali pay for any daycare or preschool as he had promised in his agreement.

And nothing lasts forever!

ON MAY 30TH 2006, ALI discovered that Noah was using Oxi's again and called his mother to inform her of the concerns. His mother replied, "My son is not doing drugs! You're mistaken! How dare you call me with such allegations!"

The woman was so defensive and in total denial of her precious "good son" having a problem, and lashed out at Ali for having the audacity to demean his character to her.

The next day, Ali and Noah broke up again.

WHEN SOMEONE LOVES AND CARES about a person they know is addicted to drugs, they may try to get that person help or try to get them to stop, but the addict has to want the help, instead of living in denial of the problem.

The desire is always there to get help for them once the problem is discovered. But an addiction is just that! They can't always stop without professional help, even if they want to deep inside. The battle lies within them.

They say that Opiates are the worst addiction to have. Addicts will do whatever they can to keep up their habit. An addict will lie, steal, cheat and sometimes even kill to get a fix, even if that person is a "good boy." Drug addiction is a serious problem this country is facing. Abuse of prescription medication is a huge issue that Ali is still, having to deal with to this day with Noah.

FOR THE NEXT FEW YEARS, the battle raged among Noah, his ignorant parents and Ali.

All Ali wanted to do was to protect her child from the possibilities, of what could have happened to Sophia, while with Noah in his impaired state of mind.

He had legal rights to take his daughter every other weekend, and there was nothing she could do about it. The judge had warned her that if she denied Noah his visitations, custody would switch to him. Ali was not about to break the law for any reason, so she would completely stress out every two weeks when he would show up to get her.

He never showed up looking high, but when he dropped Sophia off, he absolutely was. He had told Ali many times that he would do what he wanted and she couldn't stop him.

You can't even imagine the horrible thoughts that flashed through her mind. A mother whose only concern in her life is her child. To have to give that precious child to a person, who has said to her many times that he hated his own daughter and didn't want to be a father, was terrifying.

Then, knowing he was high on drugs and would be driving around with Sophia and not paying full attention to her, was such a helpless feeling... feelings of hopeless. I can fully understand why some women kill their exes. They get pushed into a corner and have no other way out but to attack.

Murder wasn't an option in this case, although the thought did cross her mind on many occasions. There was no way she was going to go back to jail for any reason. There had to be a way to protect her child without having to go to such extremes.

ON NOVEMBER 12TH, 2006, NOAH had called Ali again, threatening her. Only this time he told her that, when he got his child on Friday, and she would have to give him his child, it's the law. He was going to fuck her up and do things to her that no one was going to know about, and no one was going to be able to stop him."

Are you kidding me? What mother would hand her child over to someone who has just made a threat like that?

Ali immediately called 911 and reported it to the police. They helped her get a restraining order on him and, for the next four and a half months, Ali would have some form of peace knowing that the asshole wasn't going to have the chance to hurt her child.

But, four and a half months later, on March 28th, 2007, Noah's mother would go to court with him and testify that she was with her son when he had made that notorious phone call to her. She told the court that she was a witness that he never said those things. The judge believed her because she was such a credible witness (and not Ali) and dropped the temporary restraining order.

Noah couldn't believe that Ali had gone nearly five months without calling him. He was so sure that she loved him "so much" that she would take his verbal abuse. Surprise!! The little mommy wasn't going to take anyone's abuse ever again, especially when it concerned her child's safety.

He apologized to her that day while she secretly taped their conversation. He even admitted that his mother had lied on the stand and that he had made those threats to her. Ali could have gone back to the courts with her evidence to try to reinstate the restraining order and get his mother into trouble for perjuring herself, but she just wanted this war to end. She wanted peace and her daughter's father to help raise their child; not try to destroy them.

Unfortunately, his drug abuse continued and the battles pursued as well. Ali had a standard to live by and was not going to give up the fight to keep her child safe from an addict.

There were some moments of peace and many days when Ali and Noah got along. Ali knew that Noah's mother was at their home and would supervise them even if she wasn't required to, so that gave her some comfort. But she wouldn't give up the fight and give in to his addiction. There had to be a way to get him help and keep her child safe. She loved him, even when she thought that she hated him more than anyone she'd ever met.

His mother was still in complete denial. She refused to believe that her only son "who she didn't raise that way," could be a drug addict. Wake up and smell the roses, mamma!

Even the best families in the world have addicts in them!

Chapter 44

On December 31st, 2007, Noah stopped by Ali's house to celebrate New Years Eve with her and his daughter Sophia. I was even there at the time. He was so disturbingly high, that it really scared her. She had never before witnessed someone who was actually scratching himself so hard that he was literally digging holes into his flesh. He had opened sores all over his ears and ankles and arms. He was just sitting there, twitching and jumping and jerking out of control. His eyes were completely bloodshot, and his pupils were the smallest ones she'd ever seen.

Ali has a passive aggressive personality, and she was really trying so hard to be nice and not say anything to him. She hadn't seen him in a while because he had stopped wanting to visit his daughter every other weekend and was just doing his thing again.

But she just couldn't take watching him any longer. She began screaming for him to get out of her house. He stood up and she punched him right in the mouth with her tiny little fist. She must have hit his tooth because her hand began bleeding profusely all over the floor. She started yelling, "Look what you just made me do. Now I'm hurt!" He was so high that he looked completely confused. He told her he was going to the police to have her arrested for assault, but he never did. Believe me, if he hadn't been so high, she would have gone to jail that day. He just ran out of her house like a scared little boy.

The next morning, New Years Day, Ali called Noah's mother and said to her in a nice, polite voice. "Your son is going to die if you don't get him some help." His mother actually agreed with her, admitting that she knew, and told Ali that she would make sure that her son didn't see Sophia again until he got himself some help.

THREE MONTHS LATER, HE CALLED her, wanting to see his child again. He told her that he stopped using and was clean. Things slowly went back to normal. He was taking her on his weekends and all seemed to be going well again for an entire year. His mother, now aware of his problem, began supervising (to some degree) and life went on.

Until...December 29th, 2008, when Ali noticed that Noah had been getting high yet again. He admitted to her that his mother really wasn't supervising him with Sophia. She was just trying to appease Ali and keep her from worrying.

In the meantime, Sophia had told her mother, "Daddy took me to his friend's house to get some pills for his headache." Now he was taking his child on drug runs to his dealers? This was too much! What the hell was she supposed to do now?

DYFS had become a worthless organization to her. She had called them so many times in the past but with no success. She had to try at least one more time to protect her child, even though the courts wouldn't believe a word she said.

That little snake had even skipped out on a court order once to get a drug test. He walked out of the courthouse after the Judge ordered him to get a test without getting it done. As he walked to his car, he boasted to Ali about how he would get away with it, because no one cared. He was right! No one except Ali seemed to care.

So, against her better judgment, she made another call to the Department of Youth and Family Services.

A really attractive male investigator showed up at her house. His name was Michael. Her archangel, she thought to herself. She was enamored by his Adonis presence. So, most likely out of nervousness, she began rambling off the entire story of her life with Noah, all the court battles, TRO's, whatever came to mind. I think she enjoyed the shock value of telling her stories to a complete stranger. She told him of her past, her prison record, her parole officer's rape, all the abuse, the psyche evaluations and all the bullshit that went with them.

After the investigator left her house with his head in a spin, he went over to Noah's to hear his side of the story. God knows what that investigator thought and what him and Noah talked about.

Noah and his parents presented themselves as a nice, concerned, perfect Jewish family with no problems. Noah had a steady income with a company for many years, and if he had been a drug addict, like Ali claimed, how could he have kept his job? That was his argument with them. His parents owned a big, beautiful townhouse in a nice Republican, suburban neighborhood. Ali lived in a small, two-family house in the Democratic city of Paterson. To those people, it was like living in the ghetto.

A few days later, Ali got a notice from the courts informing her that Noah had filed for full custody of Sophia, on grounds of "physical, mental and emotional abuse, isolation and drug use in her household."

Now he was playing dirty with all of those nasty allegations against her.

"That's Ok!" she thought, "The truth shall set her free!" The guilty will accuse!

FOR THE NEXT YEAR, DYFS had Ecap workers (people taking notes while they observe a parent with her child) showing up at Ali's house at least three days a week, sometimes for two or more hours at a time. Ali enjoyed their company and even offered to feed them when she cooked something good. They sent HER for drug tests and they sent HER for psyche evaluations. Noah just refused to cooperate and he wasn't playing their game at all, and they couldn't do anything about it. He wouldn't do any tests at all.

He even smashed his daughter in the face with a ball once, so hard that he put a huge welt on her cheek. Ali took photos, showed DYFS and filed charges of assault, but the charges were dropped and nothing was done about him because he said it was an accident.

Noah bruised Sophia's arm one day so badly that he left a handprint. Again, the police were called and DYFS investigated. Sophia said daddy did it, but nothing came of it.

He was physically abusing his child right in front of the DYFS organization and they couldn't do shit about it! Ali was the one under investigation because of her past and her credibility and she was being the perfect mother.

She hired an attorney, then paid for a real forensic psychologist to give her an evaluation and took pictures everyday of Sophia's life with her. Karate lessons, gymnastics, summer camp, museums, play dates. Whatever her child did, photos were taken.

In the meantime, Ali asked the DYFS workers, "Since I have to do drug testing and psyche evaluations, shouldn't he?"

The judge handling their case even ordered their own psychologist to go to Ali's house and evaluate her situation and environment, but not his. How pathetic!

NOAH'S PARENTS HAD SPENT THOUSANDS of dollars for an attorney to help their son fight for custody of their granddaughter. They actually had filed for full custody with no visitation. They wanted to take Sophia away from her mother and never even let her see that child again.

What evil people!

One Ecap worker, who had spoken to Noah's mother, told Ali (in confidence) it wasn't Noah who wanted the custody, it was his mother. She was pushing her son to fight for his child so that she could have her.

Apparently the woman had lost all of her other biological children years ago to miscarriages and stillbirths. She must not have fully recovered from all of that. Now, in her mind, her son's child belonged to her and she wanted Sophia very badly.

This is a woman who was even running her own organization for grieving mothers who were just like her, and wanted to take a child away from **her** own mother for no good cause.

The disturbed woman had Noah, but was forced to adopt her other children because she couldn't create any others. The contempt she must have felt for Ali, who was able to give birth to four beautiful, healthy children with absolutely no complications whatsoever.

What a fucking psycho bitch! Ali thought

Instead of wasting their money trying to take Ali's child away from her, they should have been using that money to put their son into a good rehabilitation center for drug addiction. Seriously!

IT WAS A LONG, STRESSFUL battle that Ali had known in her heart would happen someday. She knew that someone was going to come along and try to take her child away from her sooner or later, and she was mentally prepared this time for the fight. She wasn't some young, naive, stupid little girl that they could walk all over this time like they did years before. She was a mature, well-educated, experienced, loving mother who was doing nothing illegal or immoral in the eyes of the law. Her only weakness, or should I say flaw, was her criminal record from nearly twenty years before. She had never gotten into trouble before that time, and she hadn't been in trouble with the law since.

That alone should have spoke volumes to those investigators.

Chapter 45

On September 29th, 2009, Ali, as the defendant, went before the family court with her attorney by her side to represent her. Noah, the plaintiff, was there with his attorney to represent him and his mother and father to give their moral support or to testify if there was to be a trial.

The judge came out of his chambers and everyone stood. "Be seated." he ordered as he sat down on his throne, wearing his royal black robe. The courtroom was silent.

Even though the allegations against her were unfounded and even though she knew in her heart that she was a good mother and had called DYFS for good cause that last time, Ali still had that underlying fear that the judge was going to look at her past criminal record and punish her (once again) for what had happened to her other child a long, long time ago.

Noah just sat across the room at the other table, staring straight ahead, expressionless. Ali looked over at him and thought, "He's so fucking ugly!" She couldn't understand what she had ever seen in him. "What an ugly human being! How could he even attempt to take a child away from her mother to never let them see each other again?" Ali tried to understand and justify it in her mind. Could the drugs have really destroyed his human nature to that degree or is he naturally just a cold, uncaring, evil, miserable person?

Then Noah's attorney spoke. "Your honor, before we proceed any further, we would like to read the reports by DYFS and by the court-appointed psychologist. The judge granted him his request and the written reports were given.

One set went to her attorney for his perusal and the other set went to Noah's attorney. Then the judge adjourned until everyone finished reading the documents and he went back into his chambers.

Ali and her attorney sat alone in the courtroom at the long table on the left side. He read the reports, silently to himself, without any expression, then slid them over to Ali for her to read. After she finished reading the reports, tears welled up in her eyes. For the first time in her entire life, she had finally read something positive about herself.

As a matter of fact, she had never in her life had anyone speak so well of her. The reports had painted her out to be the most caring, nurturing, compassionate mother. There were absolutely no concerns about Sophia's health and welfare with her mother raising her, night and day to what DYFS had said about her twenty years prior. Every word written was like a new, sweet-smelling fresh flower blooming in the sun until a beautiful bouquet was created.

Ali looked at her attorney and smiled, then he whispered in her ear, "I can't wait to get these lying assholes on the stand. I'm going to have so much fun!"

He was her friend, Anton Ranazzo. She had met him when Miles Burnstein represented her in the rape case. Anton had been his assistant. He and Ali had been friends for years since then and he knew what Noah was all about and hated him for what he was doing to her and their child. He's so disappointed that he wasn't her attorney back in 1993. He insists that she never would have gone to jail if he had been there to represent her and she wouldn't have to be going though all this crap now.

Soon after, everyone had gathered into the courtroom again, and the judge came back out of his chambers.

"Have you decided on how you would like to proceed?" the Judge asked the plaintiff's attorney. "Yes we have, your honor." he replied. "My client would like to withdraw his motion at this time."

That's it? It's over?

Then the Judge ordered Noah to go with the sheriff's officer to get an instant drug test taken.

As they all stood up to walk out of the courtroom, Noah's father looked over at Ali with a real nasty look on his face and pointed his finger at her with his thumb motioning up and down like he was shooting her. "What an asshole!" she thought to herself. "The fruit doesn't fall far from the tree!"

Ali and her attorney went outside the courthouse so he could smoke a cigarette before the results came back. Everything would have changed for her that day if the test came back positive for a substance. The Judge, DYFS and all those involved would have to believe her. She would have instant credibility. Her daughter would be safe and he would most likely have to go into a drug rehab.

But Noah wasn't stupid, he had gone to court prepared for just that and the test came back negative. The Judge once again, looked at Ali as if she was the one trying to keep her daughter away from her perfect father for no good reason and ordered her to continue giving him his visitations or violate an order and have her child taken away and custody given to him.

All the bullshit and all the lies and allegations, this battle may have been won that day, but the war was far from over. She was still left with the dilemma of what to do with this drug addict being left alone to watch her child on his weekends, unsupervised. She knew he wasn't going to stay clean for long. He never could before, so what would change him now?

DYFS was finished. They closed the case and ended their involvement. Ali had actually been glad that they were involved. At least they had given her some form of false sense of security that they were lurking in the shadows watching Noah's behavior. But that's all it was, a false sense of security. He could do whatever he wanted to his child and nothing would be done to stop him.

If something happened, his mother would lie and say she was a witness and he didn't do it. Whatever it was that he might do next, and they would have to believe her, because she was such a credible witness.

What a nightmare!

Chapter 46

Noah's parents had blown their load and lost! His mother had to accept that she was no longer going to raise Noah's child. But that's Ok. She had her adopted drug addict daughter on methadone about to give birth to a little girl. Let her take that one.

Three months later, Noah had decided (once again) that he was in love with Ali. After all that he had put her through, she was still willing to forgive him. He knew that he had been wrong and he felt bad. Apparently, he did have some feelings inside of him after all. Yeah, right!

She was just lonely for a man and remembered what a great lover he had been to her. They began talking on the phone again. He asked her to marry him once again, but she knows his thoughts and feelings are as fleeting as the wind and she will never trust him again. To her, he'll always have some ulterior motive for whatever it is he does.

She knows that once they're married, and they divorce, he'll go for custody and this time she'll lose. As long as they're not married, Sophia will always have residential custody with her mother.

She has played along with him to see how things will play themselves out. But will never let her guard down when it comes to her child and her child's father.

He continued his drug use after the court battle and his parents finally got tired of defending his behavior and wasting their money. They both retired, and within a few months, they had sold their home in New Jersey and moved out of state far enough away from their son, that he has only seen them once or twice since their departure.

Noah's mother called Ali and sincerely apologized to her, but she really doesn't want to hear it. Her contempt for his parents is as black and as hard as the Spirit of De Grisogono. Instead of getting their son help they fought her to take her child away. That just showed her how fucked up their priorities really are, and she will never forgive them. All she ever wanted was some respect and a family for Sophia to have when she's no longer around to take care of her and protect her.

They even had the audacity to invite her and Sophia down to their new home. They said, "There's plenty of room." What a joke! For the years that they lived close by, not one time was she ever allowed into their home, not even when they threw Sophia her birthday parties, and Ali really resents that. If they dropped dead tomorrow, she wouldn't shed a tear. Believe me!

IRONICALLY, NOAH GOT FIRED FROM his job after a decade of working with the company and was now one of the statistics collecting unemployment. He showed up at Ali's house asking her to help him get off of drugs. She took him to a doctor who put him on Suboxin and Ali became the one to administer his meds to him. She still refuses to let Noah watch their child alone or drive Sophia anywhere without being there with them.

She doesn't trust him and most likely never will.

He doesn't sleep in her bed, Sophia still does. He sleeps on the couch where I used to sleep. Sometimes, Ali will wake up early in the morning and go out into the living room to watch him sleep. She says he still scratches and twitches and instantly breaks out in sweats. His system is so screwed up from all his years of drug abuse. She still notices his dilated pupils and bloodshot eyes at times, but he insists that he's not on anything. One night she even tried kissing him, but tasted some form of drug in her mouth and it turned her completely off, so she walked away.

There's still no proof with the courts that he's an addict, and if he moves out of her home and gets his own place, he'll have right's to take his daughter for unsupervised weekends.

He even admitted to her, that if he had to live alone, he would most surely be getting high again. Even though a part of her really doesn't want him there with them, she really has no other choice. At least with him there, she can keep an eye on Sophia with him. The eternal babysitter!

IT's BEEN ALMOST A YEAR since Noah began staying with them and he still hasn't gotten himself any professional help other than going to a doctor who put him on Suboxin. He either stops taking his meds and relapses or takes too much of it and runs out before his next appointment to the doctor for a refill.

For weeks at a time, Ali has had to watch him lying on her couch, unable to get up because he's too weak from going through withdrawals. The doctor gives him a prescription and he takes all the pills, before he should. Then he has to suffer until he figures out a way to get relief. You would think that after all the years of going through this, that he would want to help himself, but he can't help himself, he's sick. Addiction is a sickness! And it eventually catches up to you if you don't want to help yourself by getting professional help.

Poor Sophia doesn't understand why her daddy takes medication that makes him sick. And it hurts Ali to have to tell her child no when she asks if her daddy can take her bowling alone without her mommy coming along.

But the reality is that DYFS knows that she knows he's an addict. God forbid something would happen to them while alone, like a car accident, and he is found to be under the influence, which he most likely would be. Ali can be held liable again and have Sophia taken away from her and/or charged with accomplice to endangerment again. That is, if Sophia's not killed in the accident. Once again, it's a two-edged sword that Ali fears will destroy her life with her child.

She will do whatever she has to, to keep her little girl safe.

What's that saying, "Keep your friends close, but your enemies closer?"

Things don't always turn out the way you want them to in life, or maybe they do and you just don't realize it.

She has her little family now. It's not perfect; nothing ever is, but it's hers.

Sophia finished kindergarten in a private conservative Hebrew academy. But they told Ali that her child couldn't go back there again in the fall. They said, "Her behavior was to the extreme." They now want her to get psychological help and be put on medication before she can return to them. They're out of their minds!

The truth is, there were a few bullies in Sophia's class that kept picking on her. Ali told her daughter that if someone hits her to hit them back. She's not going to raise another victim. So Sophia listened to her mother and she wailed on them! The boys eventually got the message and left her alone, but at the expense of her reputation. The main boy, who was doing most of the bullying, had a mother who just so happens to work at the school and he'll be going back there again next year.

There was no way that Ali was going to put up with that kind of drama another year and she let them know it.

She also believes that they shunned her child, because she was the only one in that school whose parents weren't legally married or legally divorced from each other. You know how it is in the conservative world! And life goes on!

Sophia's Fourth Birthday

Chapter 47

Personally, I believe that Ali is the reincarnation of Norma Jean Baker (Marilyn Monroe), and this is her karma that she has had to come back to deal with. There are just too many coincidences for me to dismiss this theory from my mind.

First, the most obvious, she really looked a lot like her in her youth, but that's nothing since people resemble others all the time. Second, she told me a story once and I believe her.

She said many years ago, when her children had been taken away from her, she had gone to see a gypsy woman to find out what was going to happen to them. The gypsy told her that she wasn't meant to raise her children in this life. Then suddenly, the woman must have recognized her, because she jumped out of her seat and ran into another room to tell her family that she had Marilyn Monroe in her house. She even asked Ali for her autograph.

Ali, who had gone there with a friend, looked at him with complete astonishment, thought the woman was out of her mind, and just wanted to get out of there as quickly as she could. She really thought the gypsy woman was crazy.

But then she thought about what was said after she left, and asked her friend while they were driving home, "What if the gypsy was right? What if I had been her? That would be terrible!" Ali never had a great opinion of Marilyn Monroe. She thought the woman was kind of fat and untalented. Was she really a dumb blonde? She knew how miserable her life had been and how she had been in foster homes while her mother was in an institution. She couldn't have any children and had spent her entire life searching for her soul mate.

But at least she died a Jew! That was the only positive thing she thought of about her life. That, and the fact that she had been married to Arthur Miller the famous playwright. He was a handsome, intelligent, talented Jew.

Ok, we can't leave out the great Yankee Joe. He probably loved her the most!

But to think that Marilyn Monroe allegedly died from a drug overdose. Well that's a great role model! Why couldn't she have been someone more stable or someone happier with her life? Well, at least Marilyn was a Hollywood legend. Whoop-de-do! She couldn't take that with her when she died.

But then, after she had thought about it, and accepted the concept of being Marilyn Monroe, Ali flew out to LA, back in 1992, to do a candle burning ritual on Monroe's grave to try to send all the demons, that had followed her into this life, back into the past. She thought that a curse had followed her into this life and she wanted to break it. She really thought she'd be able to do so with her crystal ball and a candle. Ok?

She had done it on Halloween at exactly midnight at the Brentwood Memorial Cemetery. Some attorney she had met out in LA actually sat in the parking lot waiting for her to finish. Earlier that day, when Ali was at Marilyn's grave, a couple people took photos of themselves standing next to her at Marilyn's spot in the mausoleum. Apparently she had also made the newspapers all the way out in Aurora, Colorado, where her friend lived. He had called her and told her that her picture was in the paper. It read that there was a Marilyn Monroe running around Hollywood. That's pretty interesting!

BEFORE ALI HAD GONE TO LA, she had her hypnotist friend put her under hypnosis again to find out if any of it was true.

She recalls being in a house, in a bathrobe, hearing the doorbell ring. She went to answer the door to find two men standing there. They said, "We've come to get the book that Bobby had left here." She walked into her bedroom to get, what appeared to be, a red book that was sitting on her nightstand next to the bed. She opened it to find what looked like a business ledger, with a lot of numbers and dates.

One of the guys, named Anthony, said, "You must be the Marilyn everyone is talking about. Then he pushed her down onto her bed and held her hands over her head while he tried to unzip his pants. He was going to rape her. He reached down to kiss her mouth and she bit him really hard on his lower lip. He just smacked her across the face really hard and called her a "Fucking bitch!"

His other friend, who was standing in the doorway watching him, said, "lets just get out of here." Then Anthony, a big man, wearing tan pants and a white shirt while still sitting almost on top of her reached into his pocket and pulled out a syringe. She began kicking him and fighting to make him stop, but he managed to stick the needle into the lip of her vagina while she was kicking at him. Then suddenly, she felt a wooosh, and the next thing she knew, she was outside on the lawn watching the paramedics carry a stretcher out of the house with a sheet covering it.

She remembers hearing the sound of a dog barking and the static of a police radio. Then she saw a white poodle running around the yard.

She recalls the feeling of a cold metal comb being brushed through her hair as she lie on a cold metal table, and a woman saying out loud "she was a beautiful woman."

Then, lots of sadness and tears coming from the people who only thought that they loved her, but never really even knew her.

She was so glad to be out of that unhappy, lonely life and looked forward to the next one. She hated the sound of her wispy voice that wasn't even really her voice at all, it was just part of the character she had been living everyday, all day long. She thought to herself, "What a stupid voice. Thank God I don't have to do that anymore!"

To think, that Bobby had something to do with it all. Well,

whatever he was involved in killed him and his brother also, so she probably shouldn't hold a grudge against them.

I guess because she was an addict in that life, she loathes drugs in this one. Maybe her punishment for making so many people sad in that life because of her addictive behavior is to have to deal with addicts in this life.

For years Ali thought she was going to be murdered by an Anthony in this life, but so far, she's still going strong.

The gypsy woman told her she would be married three times in this life. She still has one more to go.

Since she wanted children so badly in her other life, she was able to have four of them in this life.

Makes sense, if you believe in reincarnation.

If you don't, and you refer to the DSM IV, that story would most likely fall under some form of a delusional created fantasy of some sort.

So, for me to believe it means that I must be suffering from delusions of grandeur myself, since I've been living with the ex- Marilyn Monroe for the past decade, who I believe has psychic powers and the ability to make things happen with only a thought.

Ali has admitted to me many times, that she was Marilyn in her past life, but if someone is to ask her, she'll laugh at them and tell them that they're out of their mind and deny it. She doesn't want anyone to know her little secret. Who knows, maybe we're both crazy!

Chapter 48

I don't care what anyone might think or doubt. I am a witness that Ali has some kind of unusual special abilities that some might call being psychic or having ESP or something. These stories are true what I am telling you. In the years that I hung out with her, some of the strangest things happened that couldn't just be chalked up to coincidence.

Once when I took her to the movies, she was acting very strange which wasn't unusual for Ali. She didn't want to watch the movie when we got inside the theater and threw her pretzels I had bought her on the floor refusing to look up at the screen. I begged her to stop being so selfish. I really wanted to see the flick. Ali told me she wanted to get her money back and go home, that the movie sucked. She eventually looked up at the screen and starred at it for just about a minute when suddenly, right before my very eyes, the film melted and the movie got cancelled. Everyone in that room either got a rain check or got their money back. I called her Fire Starter and told her that I was going to tell on her. That what she did was very bad. She just laughed at me and told me that no one would believe me anyway.

Another time, there was a car parked in front of our house where Ali liked to park her car. One day we came home and the car was in her spot. Ali said to me, "I wish that car would just blow up!" A few days later, around 5 AM while we were sleeping, we heard an explosion outside, right in front of our house. Ali jumped out of bed and ran to the window to see what had happened. She started yelling that a car was on fire then called 911 to get some help in putting it out. She was worried that the fire might hit a gas line and blow up the entire block. It happened to be the car she had complained to me about. Once again I called her Fire Starter and told her to stop doing those kinds of things. Even her own mother has reprimanded her on occasion for things that no one would ever believe was possible to make happened by just thinking about it.

ONE DAY, I HAD TAKEN a ride with her to see her psychologist. As we were leaving the parking lot, Ali said to me "Let's take a ride and let the spirits lead us to where we need to be." She began to drive us through the town of Oakland. I told her that my friend Forrest Capon lived there with his family. She said, "I wouldn't want to live here. I sense that there are a lot of accidents." I reminded her that there are a lot of accidents everywhere. She said "No, I feel them here."

We continued to drive until we got to Route 23 south and then she said, "Let's stop at this diner, I'm hungry." She pulled into the parking lot of the Route 23 Diner. When we walked inside, she suddenly gasped. I asked her what was wrong and she told me she just saw a ghost. She said the image she saw was like the shadow of a big man wearing a hat. Then she said she had to throw up and ran to the bathroom gagging. She hadn't eaten anything that day so she found herself dry-heaving into the toilet.

After she was finished, she started towards the bathroom door when a waitress entered. Ali asked her if someone had died there recently and the woman looked at her as if she were crazy and replied, "Not here honey, maybe somewhere else." Ali told me she was losing her mind again because she believed that she saw the spirit of a dead man in the diner. She said that the energies the spirits give off are so strong that they make her nauseous.

After we had eaten, we took a ride to the Burlington Coat factory. Ali loved walking around clothing stores. She said the different colors and styles of the clothing stimulated her sensory perceptions and eased her mind. I waited in the car for her while I read the local newspaper.

It blew my mind when I got to the Obituaries and read that my friend Forrest Capon had just died in a car accident. We went to investigate the sight of the crash the next day and I aimlessly walked around looking through all the broken pieces of busted up car and glass hoping to find some significant remnant that might have belonged to him. Ali was just sitting in the car waiting for me when she decided she would have to wait all day if she didn't help me.

I watched her get out of the car and pick a stick up off the ground. She brushed it across a small area of grass back and forth then dropped it and headed towards the road. She began kicking the debris that had accumulated against the curb while I looked elsewhere.

Suddenly, I felt a tap on my shoulder and turned around to find Ali holding in her hand a large gold ring that had the image of a Trojan head on it. I immediately grabbed it from her and said, "This is my friends ring!" She screamed for me to give it back, that she had found it and it was hers to give back to his wife. But I wouldn't give it back to her so she began punching and kicking me. We were actually fighting over a ring in the middle of a crash site on the side of a highway. Eventually I agreed that we would both give it back to his wife if it belonged to Forrest and if it didn't, I told her I would let her keep it.

When we got home that evening, I called Forrest's wife and asked her if he had been wearing a ring when he died. She began crying and said that he had lost it. Then she described it to me. Ali had found his ring. We returned it to his wife that very night. She even showed us a photo of her husband wearing the ring.

I told his wife that Ali was a psychic and she thanked us both for finding it. Then, she invited us to the funeral and the gathering that followed. It was held at the famous Brownstone in Paterson.

Forrest had been a police detective for many years, but he also sang in nightclubs on the weekends. His wife told us that

1

Randy A. DeOrio

he had just finished performing at a bar and was on his way home. It was around 3 AM. He had stopped at the Route 23 diner for a cup of coffee before returning. That was the last place he had been before he hit a huge buck on the highway that caused his accident. Forrest *was* a big man and I believe that it was his spirit that Ali had seen that day in the diner.

FOR AN ENTIRE YEAR ALI couldn't go into large buildings out of fear something bad was going to happen. This was back in the year 2000 and is documented by her psychologist. She was waking up in the middle of the night complaining that she was going out of her mind. I spent many nights in the emergency rooms with her while she suffered from some sort of anxiety disorder. She couldn't even go into a mall without feeling claustrophobic. Running back out to her car either vomiting or dry-heaving in the parking lot. She began putting Tattoos all over herself that year. One of them was of Dracula. She kept repeating to me that, "He had honor!" Whatever that meant.

WE HAD TAKEN A TRIP to Florida in the year 2001 to visit her father who was dying of bladder cancer at that time and was supposedly on his deathbed. When we got to her parents home, Ali began massaging her father from head to toe and feeding him. I remember hearing him say to his wife "Ma, she's a professional!"

After a few days he was happy to be out of bed and walking around again. Ali's sister's actually got angry with her and said, "Why did you bring him back to life? He was going to die and rest in peace. Now he's going to live and continue making us all miserable." What fucking bitches! She thought. Ali loved her father and believes that because of her visit, he got to live another six months.

She told her sisters before we left that they were both crazy, than said to me, "Let's get out of here Randy! These people are all insane." Her dad had thrown everyone out of his house accept me. He liked me! Ali wanted nothing to do with visiting her family after that.

We stayed about a week and while leaving Florida, she

:1

wanted to drive across the states to New Orleans, so we drove to Louisiana and spent the day in the French quarters.

Ali had once read a book about a family of witches from New Orleans and told me that the author's descriptions were so vivid that we followed her memory of them while we walked and they actually led us right to the author's house. There was a limo parked in the street, so we rang the doorbell and got an autographed photo of the famous author that day. Ali is amazing!

WE DROVE THROUGH PENNSYLVANIA ON our way home and got back September 10th 2001. That night, she woke up at 4 AM screaming that she was on fire and that she couldn't breath. She was frantically pacing the floor holding her head yelling for it to stop. I really thought that I was going to have to call the paramedics for her. I figured that maybe she was having a mental breakdown because of her father. I told her to calm down that she had been through this before and it would pass.

She yelled at me, "You don't understand! Something really bad is going to happen! I can feel it!" I reminded her that something bad happens everyday. She screamed, "**YOU DON"T UNDERSTAND**! Something **REALLY BAD** is going to happen!" I said, "Ok. Lets just try to focus. Maybe we can figure it out. Is it your father? I asked her. "No!" she replied. Is it your mother? "No!" I went through all of the people we know including ourselves, then said to her "If it's no one we know and not us, it can't be that bad, so try to go back to sleep." She thought about it for a minute and agreed. Then she went back into her bedroom and fell back to sleep.

At exactly 9 AM she was awakened to a thought that she had to go on the Internet to search for blue butterflies, whatever that meant, and so she did. On her computer screen, she noticed a caption with a photo of a plane hitting the World Trade Center and read that it had just happened fifteen minutes before.

She woke me up demanding that I turn on the TV to watch the news. As she sat on the edge of our coffee table in the living room, we both watched the entire event unfold before us. She said, "This is what I've been feeling for the past year." It was like a heavy weight had been lifted off of her shoulders when it was over. She was instantly cured and no longer feared going into malls or buildings again. Amazing!

For a few days after it happened, she kept crying endlessly insisting that she heard people still trapped in the rubble. She said she could even hear the sound of a baby crying and wanted to help get them out. But there were thousands of tons of metal burying them. A couple days later, she couldn't hear them any longer.

As I watched the events of 9-11 happen that day, I told her "This is a horrible tragedy! Probably one of the worst things that was ever deliberately done to this country!" She just stared at me with an angry expression and sarcastically replied "What? Something bad happens everyday." She was repeating what I had said to her the night before when I didn't take her seriously.

She said that's why she had gotten the Tattoo's. She was trying to express something deep down inside. That's what she must have meant by Dracula having honor. Apparently he had fought against the Muslim Turks to keep their religion out of his kingdom. Maybe he was onto something five hundred years ago, But he was no roll model himself with all the people he impaled. This entire world is insane! Why can't everyone just live in peace and stop trying to kill each other?

Ali has never put another Tattoo on her body since. She feels that she is carrying the scars of that fateful day on her arms. Some people think that her tattoos are offensive, but I happen to appreciate the beautiful artful expression that they carry.

NOW WHEN ALI STARTS TELLING me that she's feeling anxiety and that it's getting worse everyday, I know that something bad is about to happen. But as soon as it does, she seems to be ok again. Her psychologist told her that its repressed emotions trying to surface, but how is it possible that she subconsciously knows when something bad is about to happen?

Some physicists believe everything in the universe, is

somehow connected by some invisible vibrating strings. They call this the String theory or M-Theory. I'm not a physicist so I can't explain this to you, but I believe that Ali is somehow sensitive to these vibrations. She can feel it when an earthquake is going to happen on the other side of our planet a day or two before it actually happens.

She once cried for two weeks straight not knowing why. She said that she just felt sad. Then when the tsunami hit on December 26th 2004 that killed hundreds of thousands of people in Indonesia, Sri Lanka and India, she told me that she was crying for all the people who had lost their children. After it was over she went back to feeling normal again.

Ali is sometimes a tortured soul that can unintentionally feel the sorrows and pains of this planet. So she hides herself away trying not to pick up the energies of other people by touching them. She says that her rock collection is a collection of orphans that were taken from their homes by man for profit. Someday they will all be returned to mother earth, when man is no longer the dominant species.

Only once in a while do I ask her to focus on a baseball game or football game for me so that my team will win. It works every time! Coincidence? I don't know and I don't care, as long as my team wins.

Here's an example... in 2005, she used her psychic abilities to make the Chicago White Socks win all four games and sweep the Huston Astros, to win The World Series. She said she was going to do it just for me, because that's my hometown. Imagine a Chicago team winning a World Series. That alone should be more than enough proof.

Isn't life great? We can create anything we want to in our imaginations and there's always going to be someone in this world who will believe it.

Chapter 49

Boxing has always been a passion of mine and I've known many boxers in my day. I once introduced Ali to the Toledo brothers, two very talented Spanish guys from Paterson who had made an impression on her. They had come over to our home once to show us their World Title and Intercontinental belts.

Ali had decided after meeting them, to show off her talents and do a painting of them that she unveiled at a benefit thrown at the famous La Neve's restaurant.

A local congressman was there with many other well-known Patersonians. Everyone loved her painting. She gave it to the father of the two brothers after the event as a gift. It now hangs in his living room.

Ali and I used to fight constantly, and I recall us having to be refereed that same night, out in the parking lot of La Neve's by the man who had once refereed the Hector Camacho / Roberto Duran fight, needless to say she won that bout as I don't hit women.

Ali is the epitome of a Bohemian if I ever knew one. She has spent a large portion of her life creating numerous works of art using many different mediums. She loved hanging out in our backyard working on her stained glass projects and once did a large train that took her weeks to complete. It wound up getting left at a stained glass shop in Fairfield and we have no idea what ever happened to it.

Her art has been stolen, lost, trashed, taken for granted and unappreciated for its value. Sadly, it's the story of most unfamiliar artists in this world. It's a shame that so many talented people go unnoticed for their skills.

Since 1999 to the present day, I've been the inspiration of a lot of the art she has done and now she is mine.

I gave her several ideas for her paintings, including the one of the Paterson Falls that is now hanging in my apartment. The painting is actually a registered museum piece as it once hung in the Paterson Museum. I just love Paterson!

My mother was born here and I have lived here nearly my entire life. Ali had Sophia here and she will always be a true Patersonian no matter where she travels to in her life.

Painting of the Paterson Falls

Ali created her own website "**Mystic-Origins.com**" and has been making some of the most beautiful jewelry I've ever seen. She uses Genuine Semi-Precious Stones and Sterling Silver to create them. You can see her rock collection there too. Please check it out! You'll be as impressed as I was!

She's the only person I know who will travel to the ends of

the earth for a rock! I have to admit that her rock collection is very impressive. She says that the energies from the stones are pure and powerful enough for healing and creativity. She even made me keep a Hematite stone in front of my computer while I wrote this book, it's suppose to block the electro-magnetic energies coming out of the monitor from penetrating my core being. She's truly an enigma!

THE ONE ASPECT OF ALI'S charm that has always fascinated me is her ability to be spontaneous. When she wants something, she will go out of her way to get it without any care for preparation, just throwing caution to the wind.

She once asked me if I wanted to go with her to a mall to get a Vikings Jacket. She loved their colors of yellow and purple. She thought the Vikings Football Team was special because they were born the same year she was in 1964. After realizing the only football jackets for sale in the sports stores around Paterson, were those of our local teams, she wound up driving us all the way to Montreal Canada. She just had to have one NOW.

She finally purchased the only Vikings jacket she could find which was an extra-large, after driving over three hundred and fifty miles, and she never even packed her toothbrush, she had to buy one when we got there.

She was always doing things like that. I got to the point that I was afraid to get into the car with her, out of fear we'd wind up in some obscured, off the wall place, far from home, the car would break down and we'd wind up getting stuck there, even though I carry AAA.

I don't know why she just didn't search the Internet to find one. It would have saved her a whole lot of time and money on gas. She told me once it was all about the adventure!

Then there was the road trip to Chicago she took me on to watch the Bears play the Vikings. We had to scalp tickets when we got there. She had told me that, "If it's meant to be, God will send us an angel who will sell us tickets." She actually got us into the game when some guy approached us selling tickets. She was wearing her Viking gear and I was wearing my Bears jacket and cap. The Bears lost that day and Ali yells out to the crowd "LOSERS!" Everyone just looked at her with contempt and one guy yell's out "Love is blind!" when he saw us together. That was really a great day!

SHE EVENTUALLY GAVE HER JACKET to Aydin who actually looked really good wearing it. At least it fit him! He took it back to Turkey with him.

Her spontaneity was what led her to marrying her second husband Joseph. She married him on a bet after only knowing him for four months! They were shooting pool one night at a bar and she told him about her days as a pool hustler when she lived in Florida. He knew she had just gotten out of prison only a few months before, so he probably thought she was out of practice for him to take such a bet. She said to him "Let's wager a little bet. If I win this game you have to marry me tomorrow." His reply was, "Ok, and if I win, you have to have sex with me in a Police Station." Apparently he was either extremely reckless or had such great confidence that he would beat her to say something like that, or maybe he just really wanted to marry her. Needless to say, she ran the table and won hands down. He had gotten his one chance on the table and blew it. I guess she hadn't lost her touch after all.

When they left the bar that night, he rented a hotel room where she gave him a private bachelor party. In the morning, he told her he was going home to get ready for their big day. After a few hours of MIA, she called his cell phone and he answered it by singing the Wedding March to her. She asked him where he was and he told her he was at work. He was the head principle of a charter school for children with behavioral problems. Go Figure! Ali got really upset and called him a liar. She told him she didn't want to see him any more for doing that to her. Apparently, he had thought they were just playing. After he realized she was serious, he gave into her whim and married her a week later.

Chapter 50

Nothing in this world that Ali has done or created means more to her than the creation of her children and their safety.

She sold her motorcycle and gave up riding when she got pregnant, but that's a good thing! She gave me a ride on the back of her motorcycle once and nearly killed me! She said, "Just hold onto me." It was like holding onto a feather.

She sold her parrots that she adored, because she felt they were too dangerous to have around her child. Parrots can become very jealous when they have competition.

When we brought Brooklyn (nicknamed Pookie) into the house eight years ago, Isabella, her Scarlet Macaw, began biting Ali very hard. It became impossible for Ali to handle her any longer and she had no other choice but to sell her to a friend.

Even though the other birds weren't as jealous, their beaks were still considered weapons that could really do damage to a child when provoked or even accidentally, Ali didn't want to take a chance with them. She's still very paranoid about everything that could cause potential harm to her child. Would that be maternal instincts or just being too overly protective? As a man I'll never quite understand the full nature of mothers, since mine abandoned me when I was twelve, but that's another story!

She finally let me take Pookie when I moved out because her beautiful white dog became my sweetheart and I can't live without her. Ali eventually got another poodle for Sophia. She calls him Shadow and he's as crazy as his mother!

Ali's desperation to protect her youngest child finally led her to the writing of an email to the Governor. DYFS got involved again which led to a court order.

Unfortunately the order was against her and Noah. Noah eventually admitted to the agency of his long-term substance abuse and is presently seeking help. The matter is still in litigation.

It seems that Noah is her destiny. He does have those beautiful green eyes and dark curly hair like she had seen in her visions. But his hair is not long, he's not a musician and he's not perfect, the way she had dreamed her soul mate to be.

The Devil is always knocking at her door with the knowledge of her past to try to use against her and DYFS is still in her life waiting for a slip up to take her last child from her. Maybe they are waiting for an excuse and will use the child's father as the reason to take Sophia away from the both of them. That is her greatest fear! There is NO safe place to go to have a "nice, quiet, peaceful family life," only places where one might feel a false sense of security until the tragedy hits. Ali believes that most people are evil by nature, hateful and misinformed. "There will be wars and rumors of wars!" All we can do is pray to God that we can be spared in the time of trial or find the strength to fight back or endure.

They say that it's the choices we make in life that cause the outcome of our existence. But what drives our desires to make those choices?

They say we have "Free Will." If that be the case, then how are we "Predestined according to Gods purpose" Ephesians 1:11

They say that when we die, we go to heaven if we're good or hell if we're not.

Some say we return to the dust in which we came. Some say we're reincarnated. Some wait for the resurrection, some don't even care what happens.

No one really knows! Why are we here? We make choices according to our options. But there is a powerful driving force that keeps the entire universe flowing endlessly, night and day,

Patea al patán de tu vida

¡Que nunca más jueguen contigo!

por Liz Aimeé Hernández

Order this book online at www.trafford.com
or email orders@trafford.com

Most Trafford titles are also available at major online book retailers.

Estudiante de Doctorado en Psicología en Consejería

Printed in the United States of America.

ISBN: 978-1-4269-4774-2(sc)
ISBN: 978-1-4269-4775-9(hc)

Library of Congress Control Number: 2010916663

Trafford rev. 02/28/2011

 www.trafford.com

North America & international
toll-free: 1 888 232 4444 (USA & Canada)
phone: 250 383 6864 ♦ fax: 812 355 4082

black and white, good and evil, negative and positive. Just when we begin to think that we're safe in the light, darkness befalls us and we suffocate! Breath! "Out of evil comes good!"

And life goes on... Until Tomorrow!

A Drawing By Sophia- 2010

About the Author

Randy DeOrio was born in Chicago, but raised in Paterson New Jersey. He was an award winning boxer and a full contact karate tournament fighter. He is a licensed boxing trainer in both New Jersey and Pennsylvania.

Has done executive protection as an armed guard and has worked as an Expert witness for many police departments throughout the New York and New Jersey area, supplying discovery evidence to prosecutors for speeding Cases.

Randy has acted on both stage and in film and has played a court reporter in the television hit series Law and Order. He has also played an FBI agent in Fight The Panda Syndicate, which has recently been entered into the Sundance Film Festival. He has worked on location for HBO's hit series Sopranos. This is his debut as an author. He is currently pursuing an acting career.

If you would like to contact him or just send him your comments, you can Email him directly at... **RandyDeOrio@ gmail.com**

He looks forward to hearing from you!